P9-DEO-798

Strategic Leadership in Academic Affairs
**is made possible by a generous grant
from the James S. Kemper Foundation.**

This publication is intended to inform debate and discussion, not to represent or imply endorsement by AGB or its members.

Copyright © 2002 Association of Governing Boards of Universities and Colleges, One Dupont Circle, Suite 400, Washington, D.C. 20036. Printed and bound in the United States of America.

All rights reserved. No part of this publication may be reproduced or transmitted in any form or by any means, electronic or mechanical, including photocopying, recording, or by any information storage and retrieval system, without permission in writing from AGB.

To order this or other AGB publications, call the AGB Publications Department at 1-800/356-6317 or visit the association's Web site, www.agb.org. AGB members are eligible for bulk discounts.

Contents

Foreword   **vii**

Acknowledgments   **xi**

Introduction   **xiii**
Season of Hope, Winter of Discontent   xiii
The Approach   xv
A Summary of Contents   xvi
Scope of the Work   xviii

Chapter 1
The Culture of Academic Decision Making   **1**
Tension in Values   2
Autonomy Versus Control   3
Love of Knowledge and the Burden of the Practical   4
Finding Shared Values   5
Decision Making and Leadership   6

Chapter 2
Teaching and Learning in an Era of Transformation   **11**
Universal Higher Education   11
Teaching and Learning   12
Engaged Learning   14
Information Technology   15
Internationalization and Multicultural Studies   16

Chapter 3
The Strategic Structure and Evaluation of Academic Programs   **21**
General Education   22
How Trustees Can Monitor the General Education Program   25
Academic Majors   25
Professional Studies   27
Interdisciplinary Studies   28
Graduate Programs   30

Research   31
Student Development   33
Enrollment Planning and Management   34
Assessment   36
Program Review   40
Accreditation   40

Chapter 4

Strategic Analysis of the Academic Budget   **43**
Planning and Budgeting   44
Financial Models and Information Systems   45
Responsibility Center Budgeting   46
Tuition Revenues and Financial Aid   47
Containing Academic Costs   48

Chapter 5

The Dynamics of Trustee Responsibility   **51**
The Decision-Making Process   53
Case Study: Crisis in General Education in a Liberal Arts College   55
Case Study: Academic Exigency   59

Chapter 6

Faculty Responsibilities and Tenure and Appointment Policies   **61**
Tenure, Academic Freedom, and Security   63
Tenure and the Elimination of Mandatory Retirement   65
Alternatives Within Tenure Policies   66
Tenure Quotas   68
Temporary Appointments   69
Part-Time Faculty   69
Post-Tenure Review   70
Early Retirement   71
Alternatives to Tenure   73
Tenure Process and Procedures   74
Promotion   78
Faculty Development   78
Statistical Profile of the Faculty   79
Monitoring Faculty Policies and Procedures   80

Chapter 7

The Academic Affairs Committee   **83**
The Work of the Committee   84

Case Study: Problems in Academic Advising at a Regional State University   85
Program Approval   87
Faculty Personnel Policies and Decisions   88
Committee Membership   89

Conclusion   **93**

Bibliography   **99**

About the Author   **105**

Appendix I   **107**
**Results of an AGB Survey on the Board's Responsibility
    for Academic Programs**

Appendix II   **119**
Advisory Group to the Academic Affairs Project

Index   **121**

Foreword

The most ambiguous governing board responsibilities concern academic program quality and faculty personnel policies. These areas are the very heart and soul of the higher education enterprise, yet many academic leaders presume them to be beyond the purview of most lay trustees. Board members who serve on the academic affairs committee often find the experience more frustrating than satisfying, more mystifying than clarifying, more limiting than consequential. This unfortunately extends to their colleague trustees who do not serve on the academic affairs committee. These individuals look to committee members, often naively, for assurance that the institution's academic health, policies, and reputation are being successfully monitored and appropriately influenced.

The purpose of the substantive and timely work that follows is to reduce the inevitable ambiguities that accompany the board's policy responsibilities for academic affairs. Because an institution's success in the marketplace depends largely on the reputation of its academic offerings, it is essential that governing boards engage *appropriately* in the many vexing issues and options the institution confronts. Boards have legitimate concerns about academic program quality and faculty work, and trustees properly expect to participate in the difficult decisions affecting these matters. For offering a strategic and practical route through the academic minefield, we are indebted to Richard L. Morrill, president emeritus of the University of Richmond.

His book is timely because some boards have gone well beyond the reasonable bounds of responsible trusteeship by making ideological intrusions into curricular decisions—even to the extent of dictating course requirements. That boards have the legal authority to do virtually anything they collectively decide with regard to academic offerings and faculty matters is a fact. But it also is true that exercising prudence and restraint is as virtuous as having the courage to insist on change where it is needed. Respecting the academic culture, even with its imperfections, is no less important than recognizing that governing boards have their own shortcomings. *How* policies and practices are changed in the academic thicket is at least as important as *what* is changed.

This book advocates collaborative leadership exercised at the nexus of academic affairs, institutional budgeting, and strategic decision making congruent with the institution's mission.

Two other important AGB publications are relevant to the issues addressed in this book: the "AGB Statement on Institutional Governance" (1988) and "Governing in the Public Trust: External Influences on Colleges and Universities" (2001). The first searches for the proper balance with regard to faculty collaboration in institutional governance, and the second addresses the board's relations with the institution's diverse stakeholders. We commend them to you.

Meanwhile, we acknowledge the fine work embodied in this book's predecessor, *Trustee Responsibility for Academic Affairs*, by Richard P. Chait and Associates. For more than 18 years, this book provided useful guidance to hundreds of boards and thousands of trustees in private and public higher education. Since it was published in 1984, however, higher education and society have changed dramatically, and the issues and options affecting the academic rigor and reputations of colleges and universities are more challenging than ever—thus the need for appropriate trustee and governing board engagement and this new book's advice on how to do it responsibly and effectively.

Read cover to cover, this book offers an elegant argument for strategic leadership in academic affairs as a collaborative enterprise of the faculty, administration, and board—especially but not exclusively through its academic affairs committee. Indeed, the committee has a special calling to help the chief executive and chief academic officer help all trustees better understand and articulate the institution's academic strengths, weaknesses, and strategic priorities consistent with its mission and financial capacity. Each chapter provides key questions for trustees to consider as they address academic policy. The index provides the means of quickly finding information on various topics. Data from a 2001 AGB survey on the board's responsibility for academic programs offer comparative and benchmark information on current policies and practices. A portion of this survey appears in Appendix I, and highlights appear as "Data Points" throughout the chapters, like this:

DATA POINT

89% of respondents from public institutions said it is important to change admission standards to alter the composition of their student bodies; **53%** from private institutions said so. In 1984, **40%** of institutions called this important; in 2001, **60%**.

Whether read straight through or selectively, this book is a gold mine of useful ideas and concepts that can help trustees monitor the institution's effectiveness. Selected chapters can serve as the focal point of discussions at committee and board meetings, for example, or at joint meetings of faculty leaders and academic administrators.

Author Richard L. Morrill brings to bear nearly 20 years of experience as president of three independent institutions. He has served on several boards of trustees in the private and public sectors. A widely published author on values and ethics in higher education as well as a frequent speaker on strategic planning and academic leadership, he is an eminently qualified and gifted writer, as you will see. His talent and enthusiasm for addressing difficult academic issues make this a useful and practical volume. We are especially appreciative of his openness in accepting ideas from others who have had the privilege of working with him on this project.

Our gratitude extends as well to the members of a distinguished advisory panel who provided counsel and direction. Its members are listed in Appendix II. Finally, very special appreciation goes to Thomas Hellie, executive director of the James S. Kemper Foundation. The foundation's generous gift made this book possible. The Kemper Insurance Companies and the foundation are exemplary members of the corporate philanthropic community.

Please let us hear from you as you use this book in the course of your work. Rich Morrill joins with us in encouraging you to share your experiences and suggestions for improving future editions.

Richard T. Ingram
President, AGB
Washington, D.C.
March 2002

Acknowledgments

Some months ago, Tom Longin, vice president for programs and research at AGB, and a respected colleague from earlier common involvements, asked me to consider writing a book on the governing board's responsibilities in academic affairs. The book would be the centerpiece of a larger project that would include an opinion survey, interaction with an advisory panel, and the development over time of new programs in AGB's ongoing work.

Tom's confidence in me led to a rewarding collaboration with other AGB leaders including President Tom Ingram, Executive Vice President Rick Legon, and Vice President for Publications Dan Levin. Each of them expressed enthusiastic support for my involvement in the project, and I thank them for it.

Susan Whealler Johnston, AGB's director of independent-sector programs, coordinated the project and has been a splendid partner in the preparation of this text. Both insightful and gracious, Susan has offered good counsel, good humor, and steady support. I am grateful to Tom Longin for his faith in my ability to make a contribution to the project and for Susan's skilled assistance.

AGB's highly professional staff includes a fine editorial team led by Dan Levin. Dan himself and his colleague charged with oversight of the book, Senior Editor Susan Shoulet, have been excellent collaborators, as has Senior Editor Charles Clark. They have shown thoughtful appreciation of my efforts, but also have given the text more vitality and clarity than it otherwise would possess. I also am grateful to Barbara Perkins, director of the Zwingle Resource Center at AGB, for assembling the bibliography.

Echoing throughout this essay are the voices and actions of a long procession of outstanding trustees with whom I have been privileged to work at five institutions. From my early days working under the artful tutelage of President Ted Eddy with the fine board of Chatham College, to my service as president of three colleges and universities, I have benefited from witnessing effective trustee leadership in action. At Salem College, Charles Vance and Thomas Douglas III were exemplary board chairs.

In my subsequent service at Centre College, I worked with a splendid group of trustees whose chairs during my time were James H. Evans and David Grissom. These two national business leaders provided Centre College with remarkable stature, commitment, and energy. The oft-times chair of Centre's academic affairs committee and long-time vice chair of the board, the distinguished federal Judge Pierce Lively, modeled many of the ideas I have tried to capture in these pages. My respect and affection for these Centre leaders continues unabated to this day.

During the decade I served as president of the University of Richmond, I saw firsthand how lay trustees effectively provide direction for an academic institution. Jack Jennings, Lewis Booker, and Austin Brockenbrough III demonstrated the best principles of trustee leadership as rectors (board chairs) during my years of service, and each has graced my life with their friendship. Mr. Booker, a superb academic affairs committee chair, has marked my understanding of these matters by his deep commitment to collaborative, democratic decision making.

The current board of the University of Richmond, under the knowledgeable leadership of Robert L. Burrus Jr., has provided me with the opportunity to continue to serve the university and higher education in various ways, including teaching and writing. In the professorship I now hold, created by the board in my honor, I have the opportunity to undertake projects such as this one.

Others on the university's campus have helped me prepare this text and are owed my thanks. In particular, my student assistant, Samuel Brumberg, collected and reviewed various books and other materials. He also gave the text a meticulous reading in various stages of preparation. Barbara Morgan, secretary in the chancellor's office, has patiently and effectively prepared and revised more drafts of the text than either she or I care to remember.

I am humbled by the confidence that has been shown in my work and grateful for the support I have received.

Richard L. Morrill
Richmond, Virginia and Paris, France
March 2002

Introduction

Now is an opportune time to reflect systematically on the responsibility of the governing board for the academic programs and policies of higher education institutions. Trustees themselves often confess to confusion about this responsibility. During the 20th century, the teaching and research missions of American colleges and universities progressively became the special domain of the faculty. As academic disciplines became increasingly specialized and professionalized, members of lay governing boards found themselves unable, unwilling, or unwelcome to make judgments about the complex intellectual worlds of the faculty.

Trustees typically are comfortable actively overseeing a college's building program and its financial and business operations. In these realms, an administrative structure exists with clear lines of authority and responsibility. This is a familiar world to most trustees. But as they encounter the sphere of academic decision making, they are perplexed. They perceive the administration to be deferring to faculty committees that work in slow motion on important matters without deadlines and in apparent isolation from the real world. Trustees often find collegial decision making itself to be bizarre. They wonder who is in charge. Trustees know that governance is to be shared, yet who shares what with whom on what occasions is an enigma. In their view, the system clanks along with an ambiguity that can be tolerated until the wheels begin to come off. At that point, nerves fray as administrators and trustees push the faculty for rapid responses to solve problems, develop programs, or reduce expenses, yet the academic machinery still grinds along at its own pace. Given the accelerating pace of change and challenge in higher education, it makes sense to reexamine the prevailing assumptions about shared campus decision making in the academic sphere.

Season of Hope, Winter of Discontent

Beyond the persistent and perennial problems of academic governance, new challenges and opportunities dot the higher education landscape. These realities typically stand in countervailing relation to one another, as respect for the educational enterprise is stalked by a shadow of discontent. The academic independence of higher education is affirmed, even as controls over it steadily increase. Many states provide excellent resources to their universities, yet funding increasingly is tied to a demand for performance indicators that suggests doubts about the faculty's work load and the quality of student learning. Leaders in government and business trumpet the enduring value of liberal education, even as the institutions they represent demand that colleges develop ever-narrower job training and certification programs. Proprietary and for-profit competitors celebrate their alleged successes with "learning outcomes."

At times, these tensions will worsen and unveil a deep distrust, as when a governing board mandates central aspects of an institution's academic program. The conflict between the autonomy of higher education and the requirement for accountability appears in many different forms, and it sets the context within which governing boards must fulfill their duties.

In significant ways, this is an exceptionally promising time for American higher education. Society and a technologically driven economy must have the advanced knowledge, the skilled work force, and the informed citizenry that only higher education can create. The extent to which higher education develops the ability of individuals to think independently, solve problems, reason symbolically, communicate effectively, use information technology, and fulfill civic commitments will determine the success of our society. With stunning proportions of the population seeking advanced education, we have reached the edge of the long-promised learning society. Yet with opportunity comes frustration and even anger. Perhaps it is because higher education offers such essential rewards, and is so imbued with personal and collective hope, that frustrations over educational access or disappointments about quality create such flashpoints of discontent.

Even though educational opportunity and access are at all-time highs (aided by massive funding for student financial aid and scholarships), public and private institutions alike are under constant pressure to control their costs and prices. Many believe that higher education has yet to respond decisively to economic realities by restructuring the nature of academic work itself.

Nor has higher education fared well in the way the public perceives the content of the typical curriculum. Many academic disciplines have refashioned their methods and content to incorporate the experience of groups omitted in the past. Yet even as universities celebrate their achievements in enlarging the study of diverse cultures, many critics construe the diversity movement as an effort to apply affirmative action to learning. They see the focus on cultural diversity as a misguided effort to redress imbalances in the traditional self-understanding of society. Conflicts over the curriculum have spread into the public domain and have produced counteractions to stress the core traditions and values of Western civilization. Such debates have worked themselves into the boardrooms of higher education.

The continuing clash of expectations in and around higher education reflects the conflicting messages our complex society sends. Programs, faculty, and facilities should be the best in the world, but prices must be low. The extraordinary success and productivity of the research of American universities are a standing expectation. Yet the perceived preoccupation with research has spurred a blistering critique of the university's abandonment of its commitment to teaching. Nearly everyone somehow can take advantage of a higher education, yet the standards of quality in the new learning society are suspect. Members of our work force need a basic education to perform well as employees, but that education also should elevate the spirit, nourish civic virtue, and discipline the mind.

These conflicting perspectives provide the context for this study. Facing all of these crosscurrents of educational expectation, the governing board often is ill equipped to steer its way through the maelstrom. Because they are laypersons in the academy, trustees come to know it both from the outside and the inside. Indeed, one of their principal responsibilities is to represent the public, ensuring that the institutions they hold in trust serve the common good. As they faithfully do so, trustees often sympathize with some of the critiques of higher education. They are variously amused or troubled by the laborious pace of change in academic programs. Some of the most knowledgeable and penetrating critics of tenure serve on university and college boards. They ask, with others, why we have no measures of student learning. They wonder why we affirm teaching but reward only research.

Even as they press these questions, trustees realize that academic professionals require a large measure of autonomy to do their best work, and they take pride in the exceptional achievements of many of their faculty. Trustees also feel bound to put the bona fide interests of the whole institution before all special interests and to protect it from ideological or partisan agendas. Precisely because they stand where they do, they can interpret the world and the campus to one another. As this text argues throughout, to fulfill their stewardship effectively, the board must understand, monitor, evaluate, and exercise responsibility for the institution's academic programs and policies.

The Approach

One goal of this account is to give trustees useful information to help them perform their duties. Much of the narrative is intended to provide trustees with a summary and interpretation of the academic culture and of important trends in teaching, learning, academic programs, and faculty policies. Few trustees have the time to stay current on the broad curricular trends and pedagogical methods taking hold on American campuses, so this summary is an effort to provide explanations and background information. It represents a scan of the academic environment, which is one of the important steps in strategic thinking about any educational issue. Even though these specific issues will change over time, the overall discussion exemplifies the kind of information that assists trustees as they exercise responsibility in the academic sphere.

Beyond providing information, this study seeks to provide a perspective that will make the trustee role in academic affairs more vital and effective. That perspective is developed principally in the early parts of the book and reappears frequently throughout the text. Its central tenet is that the board's responsibility for academic affairs should be considered in terms of the board's participation in the collaborative strategic leadership of the institution. This thesis emerges from a variety of sources, including an interpretation of the culture of decision making in higher education. Although it is consistent with traditional understandings of the faculty's primacy in curricular matters, it opens new possibilities for collaborative academic decision making on the part of trustees. Trustees not only need information, they also must have a clear sense of how to make use of it.

The third major thrust of the text consists of suggestions, proposals, and tacit and explicit recommendations about how trustees should carry out their duties to understand, monitor, evaluate, ensure accountability for, and make decisions about academic programs and policies. The proposals are many sided and range from suggestions about questions trustees might ask to data they should be provided. Sometimes these proposals are specific; at other times they offer a general orientation to inquiry. In several places, case studies illustrate the possibilities of board involvement. Most of the suggestions and ideas derive from the existing literature of proposed "best practice" that is found in a variety of materials, especially those published by AGB.

The presupposed framework of shared governance in academic matters is largely consistent with the classic documents in the field, such as the 1966 "Joint Statement on Campus Governance" adopted by the American Association of University Professors and commended for the consideration of their members by the American Council on Education and AGB. Recent AGB policy statements, the "AGB Statement on Institutional Governance," published in 1998, and "Governing in the Public Trust: External Influences on Colleges and Universities," published in 2001, affirm the traditions of faculty control of the curriculum, even as they clarify and restate other aspects of institutional governance—especially those related to governing boards.

So, information that trustees should know, suggestions for what they might do, and a framework for considering how they might do it are the three intertwined themes in the text.

A Summary of Contents

Chapter 1, "The Culture of Academic Decision Making," explains that the perennial conflict between collegial and managerial decision making is the expression of a basic tension between the values that characterize academic professionals, such as autonomy, and those that define organizations, such as control. The chapter argues that through a method rooted in the discovery and articulation of shared values, institutions can shape an agenda for the future through a collaborative process of strategic decision making and leadership. In carrying out their duties to monitor, evaluate, and approve academic programs and policies, trustees participate in the process and, in doing so, find a new purpose in their work.

Chapter 2 gives trustees interpretations and information about broad trends in teaching and learning in today's era of transformation. One dimension of this new era is the phenomenon of near-universal higher education, accompanied by the crystallization of various methods for engaging students in learning. The dizzying possibilities suggested by the educational use of technology also are a crucial part of the emerging era, as is education in a global and multicultural context. These trends have clear implications for every board, and several general questions are posed to guide trustees as they monitor and assess developments in their own institutions.

In Chapter 3, "The Strategic Structure and Evaluation of Academic Programs," the focus turns toward the content and structure of academic programs. These programs are defined in terms of the main components of a college degree, such as general education, the major, professional studies, interdisciplinary studies, and graduate studies. The chapter also discusses important questions regarding research and the intellectual and personal development of students. Much of the narrative analyzes developments in a strategic context and is intended to inform trustees of academic trends and best practices as they review and evaluate their own programs. The chapter also suggests questions board members may want to pose as they receive reports and deliberate on various proposals. It concludes by tracing recent developments in accreditation and the assessment of institutional performance and student learning.

Chapter 4, "The Strategic Analysis of the Academic Budget," explains the nature of the academic budget by focusing on the relationship between strategic planning and budgeting. It analyzes the special characteristics of academic budgets and suggests ways to use financial models to test strategic plans. The chapter also discusses the important strategic issue of net tuition revenue and ways to constrain academic expenses.

Chapter 5, "The Dynamics of Trustee Responsibility," draws together the implications and promising possibilities of trustee responsibilities for academic matters when set in the context of collaborative strategic decision making. When trustees are well informed, they are better able to monitor, assess, require accountability for, and make appropriate decisions about academic programs and policies. As they carry out their responsibilities within this framework, boards can make a decisive contribution to institutional effectiveness. In doing so, however, they need not invade the work that properly belongs to the faculty and the administration.

The serious problems that arise when trustees substitute their judgment for that of the faculty on academic matters are analyzed from several perspectives. The chapter contains two case studies that illustrate how a board might apply the methods of active monitoring and strategic evaluation in complex situations. It concludes by examining the provocative question of whether a board should be able to declare "academic exigency" in extreme circumstances.

Chapter 6, "Faculty Responsibilities and Tenure and Appointment Policies," explores the world and work of the faculty and examines the multiple expectations that academics face. The institution of tenure is the chapter's primary focus. It discusses several alternatives within tenure systems, including quotas, the imposition of temporary or non-tenure-track appointments, tenure review of those who hold tenure, and modifications and clarifications of provisions relating to termination for adequate cause. After a brief discussion of alternatives to tenure through long-term contracts, the chapter shifts its focus to some of the specific questions trustees may wish to raise in evaluating procedures for tenure and contract-renewal decisions. The board's important responsibility to ensure fair, thorough, consistent, and well-ordered processes for tenure and reappointment is emphasized in a review of the major procedural dimensions of peer and administrative review.

Chapter 7, "The Role of the Academic Affairs Committee," illustrates a number of the major themes and recommendations of earlier chapters by applying them to the work of the board's academic affairs committee. Through this committee, both in its own internal deliberations and in its recommendations to the full board, much of the board's responsibility for academic affairs touches ground. The tasks of monitoring, assessing, and making decisions about academic programs are tested and illustrated by the introduction of a hypothetical case study. The chapter also discusses the membership and organization of the committee and offers suggestions for it to function effectively.

The Conclusion contains an analysis and illustration of trustee effectiveness in real-life academic decision making. It examines the implications of the strategic decision-making model that has been proposed and suggests that it represents a promising way to consider the use of trustee power and authority, especially given the flaws in traditional academic governance.

Scope of the Work

American institutions of higher education are extraordinarily diverse in size, mission, sponsorship, and organization, and this diversity is reflected in the structure and functioning of their boards of trustees and regents. One important distinction in sponsorship is that between independent and public higher education. The boards of most independent institutions are self-perpetuating, relatively large (20 to 40 members), and their members often serve several terms. Although public boards are highly differentiated in size, nature, and responsibility, trustees tend to serve for shorter periods and on smaller boards. Appointment by the governor or the legislature is the normal pattern, sometimes with informal recommendations coming from the campus.

There are important differences between public boards that serve as the final authority for a consolidated statewide university or system and those that serve a single campus. The boards of the larger statewide universities usually function through staff bureaucracies, and their actual decision making addresses extremely broad policy, financial, and political agendas. At the local level of a campus in a system, there may be an advisory board with various powers, some of which have political and symbolic significance. Frequently, the ambiguity of the role and authority of local boards becomes a problem.

How does this text relate to this extraordinary range of board types and roles? The sections of the book that provide interpretation and information about educational culture and trends (teaching, learning, and academic programs) and the evolution of policies (tenure and its alternatives) should interest any trustee of a senior institution desiring a brief but comprehensive review of current educational issues. The book's argument about the ways trustees might participate in decisions through a strategic plan might interest members of system boards but would offer less guidance about how planning is carried out and monitored on a statewide basis. The presumed primary audience for the discussion of the board's strategic orientation and the various recommendations for the ways to review programs and make decisions are boards that govern a single college or university, whether public or private.

Most of the working assumptions throughout the text reflect an image of a board that not only has the freedom to do its work as it chooses but that also controls the destiny of the institution it serves. In many cases, this image corresponds most closely to the world of private higher education. The book's suggestions and recommendations do not take into account the challenges of sunshine laws and the ways they may affect deliberations over such controversial topics as tenure. Nor does the work address the dynamics of the creation of public policy for higher education or the politicization of trustee agendas and decision making that sometimes occur in statewide university boards and in some public institutions. The depths of partisanship and political infighting that occasionally develop in these contexts require a separate and quite different kind of analysis.

A few words on how this study has been created are in order. Scholarly research on trusteeship—especially research focusing on the exercise of trustee responsibilities in academic affairs—is limited. Many of the available studies have been developed as part of handbooks, guidebooks, policy statements, and other materials prepared, edited, or commissioned by the Association of Governing Boards. The 1984 AGB publication by Richard Chait and Associates, *Trustee Responsibility for Academic Affairs*, covers a number of the issues found in this work; it provides greater detail on some matters and less on others. The Chait book, other sources as indicated, and the extensive AGB materials provide a cumulative testimony to a broad consensus about effective and responsible practices in the exercise of the general and academic responsibilities of governing boards. They inform this study.

In addition to this specific literature about trusteeship, the author has consulted a variety of books and articles focused on trends in higher education, especially related to teaching, learning, and academic programs. As a regular reader of a number of higher education periodicals, and as an interested and active participant in academic meetings, programs, and special projects on higher education, the author has integrated insights from a variety of sources, as well as from personal experience.

Two other sources of advice and information relate specifically to this work. First, in 2001, AGB commissioned a survey of board members and chief academic officers to identify challenges, best practices, and common attitudes related to the work of academic-affairs committees and governing boards. Throughout the chapters that follow, results from that survey—presented as "Data Points"—give snapshots of current academic governance; in some cases, historical comparisons from AGB's 1984 survey on the same topic also are included. Appendix I provides details on the data summarized in each Data Point.

Second, an advisory panel offered many helpful suggestions about the organization of the work and the points it covers. Several members of this group also reviewed a draft of the manuscript and provided useful comments. Names of the advisory panel members appear in Appendix II.

Chapter 1

The Culture of Academic Decision Making

rustees new to the academic boardroom often experience culture shock when they encounter collegial decision making. They marvel at the patience of the president and their more experienced trustee colleagues in responding to the endless ideas, proposals, and demands that issue from a series of self-conscious constituencies. Groups who believe they have a claim on the institution include students, parents, townspeople, legislators, accreditors, public officials, alumni, staff members, and assuredly, faculty members. Other organizations, such as business corporations, know the concerns and expectations that issue from multiple stakeholders and occasionally even the public. Yet colleges and universities may be unique in providing a formal role in decision making to many of their constituencies. However poorly defined or understood, the expectation for shared decision making is a given in higher education.

There are two overlapping worlds of decision making in colleges and universities—the organizational and the academic. The experience of trustees in corporations and other organizations prepares them well for the purely administrative facets of university decision making. Preparing and analyzing budgets are familiar tasks, as are decisions relating to raising money, generating legislative support, financing and constructing facilities, installing new technologies, overseeing investments, and managing the campus equivalents of restaurants and hotels. Most staff responsibilities are organized in normal ways, involving predictable administrative duties of planning, supervision, implementation, and evaluation. The norms of managerial authority and accountability prevail.

In the academic sphere, however, things are different. This realm is perplexing to most trustees because it constitutes a separate system of decision making within the same institution. In this world, some faculty members hold lifetime appointments from which they can be removed only for serious cause. Crucial decisions on the institution's primary programs and its permanent personnel often are made separately from financial and market realities. Participation in academic decisions is inclusive, time consuming, and never ending. Many decisions seem only loosely related to explicit goals and to measurements of effectiveness and efficiency. Often, those with the authority to make decisions on academic programs or personnel (such as a faculty committee or department) do not have to answer for them as individuals or even collectively.

The analysis of the differential authority and roles of campus constituencies in governance and decision making—especially of the faculty, the administration, and the governing board—is a useful undertaking. Yet formal studies of governance, authority, and responsibility often devolve into procedural, semantic, and legalistic disagreements that are impossible to resolve. All the contingencies of authority and procedure in different circumstances can never be fully anticipated or described. Consequently, faculty members and administrators frequently end up pointing fingers at one another for perceived violations of process or prerogative.

One problem with formal studies of governance is that they cannot penetrate to the challenges and complexities of real institutions confronting real issues in the academic culture of decision making. Trustees can gain the most useful insights into campus decision making by understanding how the various participants *experience* their responsibilities. Our concern, therefore, will turn toward the tacit commitments that people bring to their responsibilities to identify the underlying values that define and motivate their decisions. In other words, it is especially beneficial for trustees and other campus decision makers to discern the values that create the culture of campus decision making. What are the defining commitments that move faculty members as academic professionals to believe and act as they do? Similarly, what values affect administrators—presidents, provosts, and deans—and board members that lead them to interpret issues and make decisions in their characteristic ways? Determining the values that drive these individuals and groups is a powerful tool in probing the roots of organizational culture.

Tension in Values

Let us begin with the example of a faculty member who is named the dean. Why is it that an individual who has been a respected faculty member and a trusted colleague encounters overnight everything from deference to suspicion to hostility from his former peers? Regardless of the qualifications and skills of the new dean, and however honorable or empathetic he or she may be, a new set of tensions defines the dean's relations with faculty members. How can this be? Many studies offer research and analyses that help us understand the underlying sources of conflict in the values that shape the decision-making culture of colleges and universities.[1] The tension stems from the situation and not the individuals, as the new dean in our example surely will see. The fact is that colleges and universities are mixing oil and water by combining the values of autonomous academic professionals with the control values of organizations.

Professionals generally resist the processes of institutionalization. The same fundamental tensions relating to autonomy and control in academic institutions flourish in other organizations built around knowledge-based professionals. Observe how physicians function in hospitals, research scientists in corporations, technology innovators in companies, and attorneys in law firms, and you'll draw similar conclusions. The autonomy of knowledge professionals fuels their creativity, so schedules and systems must be adapted to fit their needs. As professionals, they alone are able to make the decisions about how to do their work and how they relate to the other professionals with whom they must work. When the decision-making culture is collegial, these professionals perceive the managerial requirements of the organization merely as an unavoidable annoyance.

Autonomy Versus Control

The conflicting values of different campus constituencies create an unusual dynamic. We know that faculty members define themselves as professionals because they possess specialized knowledge gained through elaborate methods of inquiry learned during a long period of advanced training. Graduate study is indeed a rite of passage into a world that has its own special language, relationships, forms of recognition, and professional self-consciousness.

Autonomy is one of the central values acquired in the process of becoming an academic professional. Autonomy as a value plays out in several critical directions. It encompasses academic freedom, which provides the foundation on which knowledge and understanding are created. To have the unconstrained opportunity to pursue ideas wherever they might lead is at the core of the academic profession. The university builds its very life around freedom of inquiry. The self-understanding and the achievements of modern civilization, from science to democracy, would be unthinkable without academic freedom.

Autonomy, though, comes in other forms, including the opportunity to work independently and with fewer constraints than is normal in other organizations. Academic professionals not only need to be free to explore ideas that may be strange or unpopular, but they also must be able to organize their research or to structure their daily work according to their best judgment. The wider benefits that flow from what may seem eccentric to outsiders are evident in the creativity that produces new ideas that energize the classroom and in discoveries that may transform society.

Academic autonomy not only characterizes the work of individuals, but it also defines the profession collectively. The profession sets the standards that distinguish between acceptable and unacceptable performance. Only those who know the special language, methods, and content of an academic discipline can serve as true peers to others in the same field. This reality produces a sense of strong self-consciousness for the profession that leads to its own sense of independence. University departments give administrative embodiment to this professional autonomy and create the locus for most decisions about academic content and evaluations of professional performance. Just as individual professionals insist on autonomy in making academic decisions, so do disciplinary departments. Each department promises to all others that it will not interfere with their professional academic judgments, expecting the same conduct in return. The professional independence of each department thus becomes a collegial norm as well as a territorial boundary.

Now, as academic professionals come together in a structured organization, the drama increases, and the tension in value systems becomes apparent. Just as professionals embrace autonomy, institutions emphasize order and dependability, attributes attained by means of controls. Organizations must control—define, limit, and regulate—what otherwise would be the chaos of autonomy run amok. Budgets, class schedules, teaching loads, grading procedures, parking lot assignments—all are illustrative of a dense and ever-widening set of institutional constraints. Not every faculty member can hold classes two days a week between 10 a.m. and 2 p.m. All the controls and regulated rhythms of institutional life now become the framework within which the academic professional must fulfill his or her responsibilities. Having been socialized to many of these demands through personal and professional experience, faculty members accept most of them as a normal and expected burden. Yet the system of controls creates a constant set of tensions and conflicts whenever it pushes aggressively against the demands of professional autonomy. Should controls be exerted over course content or research, over anything that is seen to touch the academic heart of things, then the conflict becomes a deep crisis in basic values.

Although the tension varies by individual and by institution, there is nonetheless a steady and natural pressure for the academic professional to want to enlarge his or her sphere of autonomy. It appears as a desire to be free from the time pressures of committee and administrative work, to escape the ever-enlarging controls of external agencies or accreditors seeking assessment data, to simplify the demands of federal or state agencies relating to issues of health and safety, or to avoid the insistence of the university on yet another survey, study, or strategic plan. The academic professional wants to be free to do scholarly work. Most professors respond to some institutional demands with nonchalance and grace. To others, they respond with hostility, especially when they threaten the core of professional creativity and freedom. So it is that the life of the academic professional plays out within the organization.

Love of Knowledge and the Burden of the Practical

There are other value conflicts in the academic decision-making culture. All academic professionals are familiar with the clash between the intrinsic good of knowledge and the day-to-day preoccupations of the organization. The sustaining joy of a faculty member is the love of knowledge. At some stage of education, the faculty member was drawn into a compelling quest for knowledge that has all the characteristics of a true calling. Commitment to knowledge does not seek an end outside itself and needs no practical justification. The pursuit is self-authenticating. It also may happen that the passion for knowledge produces benefits for the wider society—whether in the education of the young, in the discovery of solutions to complex social problems, or in the inventions and discoveries of science and technology. The academic professional knows those things to be good, celebrates them, and encourages society to support them by building and sustaining universities. Yet from the inside, the academic professional also knows the love of inquiry and the desire to join with others in expanding and communicating knowledge.

Those with whom a professor feels the closest bond and whose work is known to be (almost) as vital as his or her own are, of course, those who are in the same academic discipline. In fact, problematic issues first present themselves when fellow lovers of truth appear as members of the same organization. All of them believe passionately in the intrinsic worth and vital importance of their enterprise. With the organization, however, comes the question of relative worth, because resources are always finite. Not every good can be equally served. Competition for resources enters the equation.

Thus the reality: Institutions are required to make relative judgments about absolute goods, to divide up differentially their forever-limited resources. Practical management and decision-making concerns press themselves into the pure pursuit of knowledge. Now the talk is of priorities, productivity, cost-effectiveness, branding, and markets. In a thousand different ways, academe knows a new rationality, that of managerial bureaucracy. Deans impose limitations on enrollments in programs that have grown too large, much to the consternation of the faculty who know that their growing field should be rewarded with more positions and new facilities. Administrators question courses that have tiny enrollments and try to discontinue them or schedule them only periodically. How painful for a professional whose work has been recognized internationally to allow the random interests of undergraduate students to decide whether a small Shakespeare seminar should be offered two years in a row. As faculty members continue to experience pressures from outside and within the academy to restructure programs, respond to new types of students, cut costs, measure effectiveness, and set priorities, the conflict with the value system of academic professionals becomes intense and even hostile. In dozens of daily moments, faculty feel the full weight of institutional control. The clash in belief systems is palpable: intrinsic versus instrumental, absolute against relative.

One other form of the tension in decision making in academe is worth noting because it has immediate implications for the board's role in tenure and related faculty contract decisions. As previously suggested, academic life is, at its best, a true calling. The sense of self and the identity of the professional are intertwined. The academic professional says easily, "I am what I do." With this strong sense of identity, the person who stands for tenure or contract renewal experiences a persistent anxiety. Detailed procedures have been developed on most campuses to guide the decision-making process, but they often appear to tenure candidates as so many ambiguous and bureaucratic procedures. Somehow they never reach the core of a person's intellectual passions and achievements. If a negative decision does come, it usually is felt as a heavy blow to an individual's personal and professional sense of self-worth. Understanding this, trustees can better appreciate why tenure and contract-renewal decisions are often so intense and why effective and fair policies are so crucial but so difficult to develop.

Finding Shared Values

Trustees who understand this academic culture will be better equipped to negotiate the inescapable tensions in constituents' values. The wonderful irony, of course, is that institutions that seem to be most creative and successful—as measured by academic achievements, reputation, and resources—have found imaginative and constructive ways to live with conflicting values. They have discovered that creating and communicating knowledge requires large doses of academic freedom and professional autonomy. They also have found the wisdom and the courage to know that rigorous judgment and careful discrimination are necessary to establish priorities. To rush impatiently to one or the other side of the values equation yields no solutions; balancing autonomy with authority creates workable possibilities.

Members of academic communities know that the culture enforces sanctions against decision makers who do not respect its traditions of balanced collaboration. Those who cannot find effective ways to press legitimate claims of authority are seen as poor stewards or ineffectual leaders. If, on the other hand, decisions are made in disregard of the process of collaboration, they violate norms that have ethical force. They are seen as illegitimate and demeaning. The balance between freedom and control has been lost. On many campuses, the system works tolerably well to keep values in balance, especially if the environment is stable and pressures for change are slight. Yet when the context turns threatening and the need for change intensifies, or if the institution chooses to extend its reach for achievement and challenges tradition, cracks in the system quickly appear. Then the haziness of shared decision making becomes apparent and the conflicts in values glaring, especially if issues of academic content are at stake. At such times, trustees are quick to note the plight of presidents doing battle over governance issues, and they become mystified, frustrated, or angry about the ambiguities inherent in campus decision making.

DATA POINT

98% of board members said boards and faculty need a shared understanding of their different responsibilities for governance of academic programs. **67%** of private board members strongly agreed with the statement. **54%** of public board members strongly agreed.

Analyzing issues at the level of value conflicts may yield sharper insights about why decision making is so difficult in the academic sphere. Nearly everyone involved in academic governance harbors some degree of skepticism about the decision-making process. The question is whether that skepticism will be healthy and create new approaches or whether it will turn cynical and lead to constant political jockeying and infighting as the way to do campus business.

Decision Making and Leadership

What, then, can be done to improve academic decision making? Many faculty members cringe when the language of business is applied without adjustment or sensitivity to the work of the academy. An analysis of the campus culture may reveal why this is so. At the same time, it would be foolish not to use powerful forms of thinking and analysis, whatever their lineage, if those tools advance the true work of higher learning.

Although often misused or distorted, strategic decision making can provide colleges and universities with a dynamic method of collaborative leadership. Strategic self-definition forces a college or university to see its programs as a series of distinctive capacities by which it defines its future within a competitive environment. It places issues of institutional identity, academic quality, performance, and effective use of resources at the heart of the agenda. To be effective as a leadership tool for setting directions in a university context, strategic decision making must be collaborative, integrative, and action-oriented. When carried out in this way, strategic thinking will draw upon the contributions of a significant cross-section of the campus community, and trustees will be an important voice in the conversation.

The heart of effective strategic decision making, especially when it is used to guide the institution into the future, is found in the narrative of the institution's identity through time. Several prominent students of leadership emphasize the central importance of the discovery and articulation of the institution's story as a critical dimension of leadership. As Howard Gardner writes in *Leading Minds*, "... the story is a basic human cognitive form; the artful creation and articulation of stories constitutes a fundamental part of the leader's vocation. Stories speak to both parts of the human mind—its reason and emotion....further, ...it is stories of identity—narratives that help individuals think about and feel who they are, where they come from, and where they are headed—that constitute the single most powerful weapon in the leader's literary arsenal."[2]

Stories, of course, are concrete and tell of the actions of groups and individuals, of heroes and heroines who have shaped the defining characteristics of an institution. The narratives, images, and metaphors of the institution's life story also carry wider meanings and convey the common values that have shaped its identity. Through discovery of the way these central values are embedded in the life of an institution, a set of common commitments can be raised to consciousness and celebrated. Let the story be told of what truly matters to a place. As this occurs, campus constituencies can articulate a shared set of substantive values that provide a common ground for decisions and narrow the gap between professional autonomy and institutional control. The shared values will embody such defining commitments as quality or service, innovation or community, and will be articulated with precision. Instead of typical empty rhetoric, these terms can be given powerful expression and distinctive meaning to create the basis for a vision—the articulation of the institution's best possibilities for the future. Academic professionals will cede some of their independence to serve an absorbing cause that requires common effort, such as academic quality, especially if it is described in ways that resonate with the authentic achievements and possibilities of the institution. The pull toward autonomy is never gone, but it is transcended by shared values that move people to the common tasks of building a great institution.

In this process of strategic thinking and decision making, trustees have much to contribute. Above all, they must assure all constituents that the process is being done well. Moreover, with the president, they are the only participants who see the place whole, from whose purview no facet of institutional life is excluded. With wholeness of their vision, they can represent a continuity of responsibility. Whether of long or short service, most trustees know the institution well through various forms of association. They also carry the authority, values, and obligations that have been defined by legal documents and enacted through history, so they should know and be able to tell the institution's story. As they look to the future, they can interpret the institution's vision to the public and to the constituencies that support it.

The effort to translate common values into comprehensive strategic directions and priorities for the institution is critical to collaborative decision making and leadership. When set in a strategic context, collaboration is a natural and necessary form of decision making. Rather than produce irresolvable and legalistic disputes about who has the authority to do what, the methods of strategic leadership enable leaders to focus on common goals to shape an institution's future. The process is complex, of course, and includes deliberation among groups, the careful analysis of data, the development of comparative benchmarks, and above all, the creation of measurable goals and methods for monitoring, assessing, and ensuring results. In practice, strategic leadership is a highly integrative discipline that draws together the often-fragmented dimensions of an institution's life. It connects planning with budgeting, needs for resources with ways to obtain them, data with meaning, goals with assessment, and the past with the future.

Conducted properly, strategic decision making can energize an institution and focus the board's duties. It offers a way for trustees to clarify their responsibilities for the academic program, which they can see in a new strategic light that emphasizes the capacities that situate the institution in the world. The way the board should carry out its work in the academic sphere receives a new and vital orientation. Strategic planning can provide trustees with the benchmarks and information to monitor and assess the institution's academic goals and the opportunity to ensure accountability in reaching them.

As they assess the decision-making culture and practices of their own institutions, trustees will want to explore a variety of questions:
- What is the state of the institution's governance system?
- Has the institution effectively differentiated the roles and responsibilities of various constituencies in decision making?
- Can conflicts over these responsibilities be resolved constructively when they arise?
- Do key groups (faculty, staff, students, trustees) within the institution have a clear sense of its heritage, identity, and defining characteristics through time?
- Do trustees know the institution's story, and can they relate it well?
- Does the institution's story influence the way it makes strategic decisions?
- If a clear and shared sense of institutional identity is lacking, what efforts have been made to bring it to expression?
- Does the institution have an effective and collaborative strategic-planning process?
- Is the planning process based on an articulated sense of the institution's core values and its vision for the future?

[1] Clark, Burton R. *The Academic Life: Small Worlds, Different Worlds.* Princeton, N.J.: Carnegie Foundation for the Advancement of Teaching, 1987. Morrill, Richard L. "Academic Planning: Values and Decision Making." *In Ethics and Higher Education.* William M. May, ed. New York: American Council on Education and Macmillan Publishing Company, 1990, pages 69-83.

[2] Gardner, Howard. *Leading Minds: An Anatomy of Leadership.* New York: Basic Books, 1995, page 43.. Gardner goes on to show how leaders as diverse as Robert Maynard Hutchins at the University of Chicago, Margaret Thatcher as Prime Minister of Great Britain, and Martin Luther King as a leader of a mass movement were able to distill the essence of the message that defined the values of their followers.

CHAPTER 2

Teaching and Learning in an Era of Transformation

For trustees to participate effectively in strategic decision making concerning the academic program, they must be aware of the educational trends that are shaping higher learning. This chapter summarizes and interprets the changes that recently have altered the nature of learning itself. Although advances in information technology continue to exert a powerful influence on higher education, other factors are coming together in the early 21st century to justify the assertion that learning itself has entered an era of transformation. The interpretation of changes in educational access and in teaching and learning also may help illustrate the type of continuous scan of strategic educational issues that should inform the governing board's exercise of its responsibilities for the academic program.

Universal Higher Education

One dimension of the era of change concerns access to learning—specifically, the question of who is to receive education beyond high school. At the dawn of the 20th century, only 5 percent of Americans went on to college, and by mid-century the figure had risen to 20 percent. At the dawn of the 21st century, approximately 70 percent of high school graduates participated in some form of higher education within two years of high school, and 80 percent indicated they planned to do so in the future.[1] College attendance no longer is tied to a single age group, as adults participate in ever-increasing numbers. With college courses and programs available in countless satellite-campus locations and through rapidly expanding forms of distance learning, education is available to the populace at any age, at any time, and in any place.

In many ways, this near-universal access to higher education is a triumph of democracy and a testimony to America's commitment to equal educational opportunity. In all of history, no society has seen the likes of it. Yet an unqualified celebration of the achievement would be premature.

Federal, state, and private financial aid, as well as tax benefits and tuition prepayment plans, put college within the financial reach of nearly everyone, but neither the message nor the reality of opportunity has yet penetrated many pockets of urban and rural poverty. Nor has the enlargement of access been matched by the availability of choice among educational options. The price and availability of higher education vary enormously, so many students are unable to take advantage of the choices that best match their ambitions, abilities, and needs.

Troubling as the continuing problems of access and choice can be, of greater concern is the uncertain quality and effectiveness of the educational experience itself. In four-year institutions, completion rates stand well below 50 percent, while in two-year institutions the rates are even lower. To be sure, attrition figures often are not as negative as they appear. They can mask the fact that today's students intend to complete programs over time as they enter and leave college in response to changes in family responsibilities, financial circumstances, location, and professional ambitions. Many students have become itinerants who choose to attend several institutions before completing a degree.

Yet even allowing for a new type of student mobility, attrition rates still signal serious problems. Students often do not find connections between their lives and the programs in which they enroll; moreover, they frequently are poorly prepared for the demands of college-level study. Nor may they find a clear or compelling rationale in the requirements of a degree. Even students who complete degrees frequently do so by avoiding serious commitment to their work. In 2000, the National Survey of Student Engagement found that 56 percent of the students surveyed spent 15 hours or fewer a week studying outside of class—less than half of what most professors would cite as the expected norm.[2] Reports from employers continually circulate that many graduates do not have adequate skills in communication, problem solving, and technology. Why does higher education not ask and receive more from its students? Why are standards not higher? The issue of quality looms large.

Teaching and Learning

The exhilarating ideal of higher education for everyone with the motivation and capacity to pursue it is within reach, yet it eludes our grasp. Perhaps we simply need more patience and determination in solving problems that largely are a function of the unprecedented level of our society's educational expectations. Stay the course and commit more resources, and eventually the quality of education will rise to match our high ambitions.

Taking the long view may help, but the era of change includes other emerging possibilities to enhance educational quality. Changes in teaching and learning long in incubation and scattered in practice have begun to take hold. For the past decade or more, educators have been rethinking the nature of learning itself. That is, *what* and *how* students learn are considered more important than the teacher's delivery of knowledge. The agenda of the learning movement is a major presence in contemporary higher education.

DATA POINT

47% of responding board members and chief academic officers said it is very important to develop a plan to assess student-learning outcomes. **37%** said it is moderately important. **64%** from publics said very important, **43%** from privates.

The concerns of the reformers are many, but they center on new ways of conceptualizing educational quality. The emerging focus is on what happens to the student in the educational experience, on what the student learns in terms of enduring capabilities, skills, values, and to be sure, knowledge. "Completing courses" or "earning credit hours," even in an elegantly elaborated discipline, is not the equivalent of a powerful education.

Teachers are essential in the process of education, but their role is changing. They focus increasingly on the quality and depth of student learning, not just the delivery of a body of knowledge. The teacher's commitment to foster the understanding of complicated information and complex ideas has not been abandoned, but it has been refashioned by the preoccupation with determining how to engage students in "powerful" learning. Such learning makes a heavy claim on the time and interest of students. It stimulates motivation and personal involvement; it connects with other learning in and out of the classroom; it provides insights and information that apply to life; and above all, it equips students with an arsenal of essential abilities and values that endure, even as information may be forgotten.

Perhaps the new focus on student learning can be best understood through a brief analysis of some major forms the new emphasis is taking in higher education.

- *Student Research.* Especially in the sciences, but appearing in other fields as well, there is a growing effort to involve undergraduate students in serious research projects, often working collaboratively with faculty. Through this kind of involvement, students learn to think and solve problems as do scholars and scientists, instead of merely reading about what they do.

- *Collaborative Learning.* In virtually every discipline, students work on projects or assignments in teams with other students, often presenting their findings collectively in a presentation or a paper. The dynamic of peer interaction is highly motivating and contributes to an increased sense of intellectual community. Developing teamwork and group problem-solving skills is an important part of collaborative learning.

- *Experiential Learning.* Students routinely have completed internships and various field experiences as part of their educations. Today, internship opportunities have expanded to many fields and are required in a variety of programs. Studies show that experiential learning has a powerful effect on a student's personal and intellectual motivation and enlarges a student's knowledge by connecting theory with practice.

- *Service Learning.* Participation in volunteer service long has been a central part of the college experience for many students. Now, through many of the protocols of experiential learning, student involvement in community service is built into assignments and courses.

- *Integrative Strategies.* In response to criticism that the college curriculum consists of unrelated fragments of knowledge, many programs now integrate various programmatic and teaching emphases. Many institutions link related courses across fields to create "learning communities." Also increasingly in evidence are capstone courses that aim to give upper division students a sense of the connections within a discipline or across disciplines. The themes of many such courses may center on issues of values or ethics, and students may discuss and analyze case studies and case histories. In addition to the discipline of *knowing*, increasing attention is given to the discipline of *deciding*.

- *Study Abroad.* The possibility is not new, but steady increases in such programs are part of the changing character and form of student learning. Whether focusing on learning foreign languages in the native country, on the study of a chosen field, or on a service project or internship, learning by living and studying in a different culture is a salient characteristic of contemporary college learning.
- *Competencies.* Course objectives and assignments increasingly are related consciously and systematically to the development of such intellectual skills and capacities as effective writing, speaking, critical thinking, problem solving, numerical analysis, integrative thinking, and cross-cultural awareness.

Engaged Learning

Common to many of these approaches is a focus on active learning, on the student as an engaged participant in the process of acquiring knowledge, skill, and capacity. The implied contrast, of course, is with the image of passive learning, in which students merely receive information provided by the teacher. In the traditional model, students memorize information and concepts and then feed them back to the professor on tests and papers. They learn and use methods of inquiry in prescribed ways in defined contexts. As active learners, however, students are agents not observers, makers of meaning and not recipients of facts.

As a consequence, many courses now require students to learn by doing—to write and speak frequently, make presentations and participate in debates, address real-life problems and case studies, work in teams on research projects, and participate in internships and service learning. To know something is to be able to apply what you have learned in other situations, find solutions to undefined problems, integrate knowledge with personal experience, connect it with professional and civic responsibilities, assess the limits and possibilities of knowledge, and be curious about new knowledge.

The strategies of engaged learning immediately convey the prospect of improved quality in higher education. How could increased motivation, enlarged interest, more time on task—in sum, real involvement—*not* improve student learning? Yet education researchers have not accepted these practices at face value but have tested them in various ways. The results of those studies confirm the self-evident appeal of pursuing involvement to improve the quality of learning.[3]

How widespread are the foregoing strategies of engagement? There is no sure way to know at this point, but judging from the National Survey of Student Engagement (see footnote 3), research by various scholars, and on several projects in curricular reform undertaken by the Association of American Colleges and Universities, it is safe to say that virtually every higher education institution offers at least some courses and programs that employ practices of engaged learning. Few institutions, on the other hand, have made these approaches a systematic and defining aspect of the experience of all students. In sum, the effort is real and widespread, but short of systematic and consistent.

Information Technology

Since the advent of the personal computer in the early 1980s, computer technology has been a constant focus of discussions on every campus. How do we respond to the opportunity? Are we using it to real educational advantage? How can we encourage faculty to use technology in teaching? How do we stay abreast of the competition? How do we pay for it? If this is truly an age of educational transformation, then information and related technologies are at the core of rapid and unrelenting change.

As trustees know from their personal and professional lives, telecommunications and computers dramatically have changed the ways people gather information and communicate. In institutions that define themselves around creating and conveying information, technology always rises to the top of the strategic agenda. The new technologies have created campuses without boundaries. Instant access to information on a global basis has changed the pace of research and altered its methods. E-mail and the Internet have made it possible for every class to be a conversation that literally never ends. Through e-mail questions and assignments, discussions and information sharing, in electronic chat rooms and bulletin boards, the very business of the academy has been enriched and intensified by information technologies.

At one level, the Internet enables active learning and enlarges a student's intellectual skills. A student who can skillfully mine the Internet can unearth valuable information and synthesize numerous resources to expand his or her knowledge. At the same time, caution is essential for students who do not possess powers of critical thinking and judgment. There are no criteria for what appears on the computer screen, and many sites and exchanges are empty, boring, or even pernicious. Moreover, just as with any source of information, the Internet can encourage passive learning in which the student absorbs information with little motivation, involvement, or discernment.

The unquestioned and stunning capacity of information technology to enable communication and provide information has moved it quickly into a central role in distance education. The residential campus itself has become the primary place where the Internet provides students with course segments or entire courses. In many institutions, students can download a professor's lectures on video through closed-circuit television or the Internet. Increasingly, the Internet has become the means for delivering college courses over large geographical distances, and millions of people now enroll in such courses. Learning through the Internet pushes distance education into a higher gear, intensifying all the traditional questions about

DATA POINT

26% of responding private-institution board members and chief academic officers said technology and distance learning were among the three most important academic issues currently facing their institutions; the figure increases to **43%** in the next five years. Nearly **40%** of all respondents placed it among the top three issues for the next five years.

the potential and quality of the educational process. Every institution should consider its options in distance education and the effects of competition from for-profit educational providers or other universities on its programs.

To be sure, the Internet helps faculty and students do interesting and novel things, but the major benefit has been greater convenience and instantaneous communication. The World Wide Web gives students access to many materials, and assignments and responses can be shipped instantly from teacher to student and back again. Yet for all their convenience, electronic communications can never systematically replace face-to-face conversations and relationships between individuals.

Today, distance learning is most readily available through individual courses or series of courses in advanced, specialized, or professional studies. A full and dramatic revolution in higher education—with comprehensive undergraduate degree programs provided at a distance through elaborate and compelling courseware and real-time visual interactivity— seems a more difficult challenge. High-quality courseware has proved difficult to produce, and the technological expertise to deliver it is expensive.

All of us can imagine ways in which some of our favorite subjects might be translated into an interactive CD or a series of segments available on the Internet. But as we envision courseware that would include the text of a Shakespeare play, as well as critical commentaries on it, layered with options to view various scenes as they have been acted in film or on the stage, we find that our imagination is exceeded only by the enormous cost of producing something of solid intellectual value and high technological quality. As we imagine constant revisions to the product as changes are needed, a sense of the challenge becomes evident.

No doubt, some stunning achievements periodically will raise the question of whether a campus—as a fixed place with its full complement of people—is needed for higher learning. In a technological era in which change will continue to accelerate, trustees will need to remain aware of that powerful strategic question. In thinking about the possibilities, however, trustees also will want to remind themselves that a total educational program includes continuing opportunities for students to interact with one another and with faculty in a community of learning. As long as educational goals emphasize inclusive personal and intellectual development, residential and campus programs will seem essential.

Issues concerning the uses of technology in teaching and learning, as well as throughout the institution, will continue to challenge higher education officials and trustees as far as the eye can see.[4]

Internationalization and Multicultural Studies

Internationalization is another force shaping both the form and content of higher education. Universities not only are responding to external realities in an environment of comprehensive global change, but they also are contributing significantly to the process of internationalization. Most campuses offer a variety of courses and programs of study that focus on international themes and topics. Small institutions often develop interdisciplinary international studies majors, while large universities offer an extensive range of international academic programs and courses that focus on most areas of the world.

One of the major strategic challenges for higher education institutions is to develop a comprehensive and integrated academic approach to internationalization. Students increasingly seek a substantial international component to their educations. If courses and academic programs are to reflect a global outlook, then faculty must be able to present the international dimension of their own work, regardless of whether they developed this capacity in their initial training. To help professors meet this expanded expectation, many institutions sponsor faculty travel seminars or similar programs to help them enlarge their interests in and understanding of international cultures and themes. Responding to the same issue of international scope in the curriculum, colleges and universities have developed increasingly diverse faculties, with significant percentages of professors foreign born or trained.

Another key dimension of an integrated approach to internationalization concerns the presence of international students on campus, coupled with opportunities for domestic students to study abroad. Large institutions, especially those with graduate programs in such fields as engineering and business, typically attract a high percentage of international students. At the undergraduate level, many international students study for a portion of their diplomas in an American institution as part of exchange agreements, which also send American students abroad. In addition to such exchange programs, many American institutions have sites and programs of their own in foreign countries. The challenge of such arrangements, sometimes called "island programs," is to find ways to develop substantial contacts with the students, culture, and educational resources of the host country.

Although not always appreciated as a strategic issue, the recent emphasis on multicultural studies reflects the effort of academic disciplines to redefine themselves in a changing world. The links between a greater awareness of diverse cultures and international education are clear. Both efforts are focused on understanding the history, experiences, values, institutions, and beliefs of diverse cultural groups. In each case, there is a need for scholars to locate and interpret neglected or unfamiliar materials and for students to enter an unfamiliar world of thought and experience.

The effort to study and understand the history and culture of groups that have not been included in the mainstream of traditional courses and texts has become controversial on many campuses and in the broader society. On the one hand, most leaders in government, business, and professional life affirm the need to create a truly diverse society that respects, affirms, and understands different cultures. The link between multicultural awareness and the democratic values of tolerance and respect is clear and persuasive. On the other hand, there are many critics of multicultural emphases on and off the campus. Some scholars and commentators see multiculturalism as an effort to undermine traditional Western values, to squelch freedom of expression by engineering a new kind of intellectual orthodoxy, and to displace the classical texts of the Western and American heritage. As a result of these contending views, members of the campus community and others in society have waged battles in ongoing "culture wars" concerning what texts and courses students should be expected to study. In a number of cases, the debate has reached the level of the governing board.

Since the first days of these conflicts in the early 1980s, much has changed. College and university programs now reflect a much broader coverage in women's and multicultural studies, for example, and many campuses require that some aspect of a student's program include the study of other cultures. At the same time, the stridency and hostility of the debate over the issue on most campuses has calmed considerably. The push for recognition, resources, and political influence, always part of protest movements, has been transmuted into the work of building new programs with broader agendas. Now it is more clearly seen that liberal education not only must involve traditional Western texts and subjects but sources and topics from diverse cultures as well. Some may still feel it essential to critique or demean the tradition or the newer fields, but most campuses have moved beyond the combativeness of a narrow, either/or perspective. All institutions face the realities of the constantly increasing diversity of American society and the imperative to find common ground and values for democratic processes and institutions.

The early years of a new century are an appropriate time to take stock of powerful strategic trends in teaching and learning. Transformations have occurred in *who* is being educated, which is nearly everyone; in *how* gains in teaching and learning are being pursued, which is through technology and by means of strategies of engagement; in *what* is being studied, which increasingly includes a global and multicultural dimension; and in who will provide the educational experience among traditional public and private colleges and universities, corporate universities, and proprietary training organizations.

As trustees monitor and assess developments in the academic programs of the institutions they serve, they may want to ask the following questions:

- What are the prevailing methods of teaching in various programs and departments? Are any of them "signature" approaches for which the institution has been recognized?
- What changes or innovations have been introduced in teaching and learning, and how do they relate to trends across higher education or in specific fields?
- How will it be known whether the changes are producing a higher quality of learning?
- What are the most significant trends concerning the use of information technology and other technologies in various courses and programs?
- How are technology and distance learning affecting us competitively?
- What programs or opportunities are available to our faculty to incorporate new approaches into their teaching?
- What are our offerings and plans in the area of distance learning, both for students enrolled in courses on campus and for students in other locations? How do we assess the quality of distance learning?
- Has the institution participated in consortial or national programs related to new approaches to teaching and learning?
- What are the central components and relevant measures of the institution's approach to international education?

- Are the institution's efforts in international education part of a comprehensive and integrated strategic approach?
- What is the institution's approach to the study of diverse cultures? Do curricular requirements include multicultural studies? How do requirements reflect the American and Western heritage?
- Are we meeting the changing expectations of students, particularly with respect to instructional technology?

[1] "Greater Expectations: The Commitment to Quality as a Nation Goes to College." *Liberal Education*, Vol. 85, no. 2 (Spring 1999), pages 19-23. Much of the flavor and many of the emphases of this chapter are drawn from this article and the Association of American Colleges and Universities Greater Expectations Project, 2000-02. Report forthcoming.

[2] Kuh, George D. "Assessing What Really Matters in Student Learning: Inside the National Survey of Student Engagement." *Change*, Vol. 33, no. 3 (May/June 2001), pages 10-17.

[3] Ibid., 13. In a large-scale and ongoing research study titled the National Survey of Student Engagement, George Kuh of Indiana University uses five benchmarks of educational effectiveness. These are the "level of academic challenge, active and collaborative learning, student interactions with faculty members, enriching academic experiences, and supportive academic environment."

[4] For a variety of perspectives on technology in higher education, see several articles from *Change* magazine: Brown, John Seely. "Growing Up Digital: How the Web Changes Work, Education, and the Ways People Learn." *Change*, Vol. 32, no. 2 (March/April 2000), pages 11-20. Merisotis, Jamie P., and Ronald A. Phipps. "What's the Difference? Outcomes of Distance vs. Traditional Classroom-Based Learning." *Change*, Vol. 31, no. 3 (May/June 1999), pages 12-17. Weigel, Van B. "E-Learning and the Tradeoff Between Richness and Reach in Higher Education." *Change*, Vol. 33, no. 5 (September/October 2000), pages 10-15.

CHAPTER 3

The Strategic Structure and Evaluation of Academic Programs

What should the board know about the content and structure of academic programs? How can it evaluate academic programs? How should the board approach academic decision making?

The answers to these perennial and difficult questions begin to fall into place when the board's participation is set in the context of strategic analysis and decision making. The institution's distinctive purposes, priorities, and goals frame the board's work. From a strategic point of view, the institution's academic programs appear in a special context and take on a new significance. Courses and programs no longer are the internal domain only of the disciplines; they are the embodiment of the institution's identity and the means by which it fulfills its purposes in a world of challenge and change.

Strategically, academic programs define what an educational institution does; they form its repertoire of capabilities. Through these capacities it makes its claim to distinctiveness and quality in a demanding and competitive environment. Academic programs differentiate the institution in the marketplace for students and constitute its largest commitment of financial and human resources. Boards and presidents can make informed decisions about the academic program only if they consider its strategic relationship with external realities and other areas of university life. Deciding what facilities to build and how to fund them, long-term financial plans, the recruitment of students, and public image and support are all mirror images of academic purposes, priorities, and programs. An integrative and collaborative process of strategic decision making gives trustees a way to understand these vital relationships and helps them focus time and attention on academic programs.

None of this suggests that trustees should do the academic work that properly belongs to the administration or the faculty. This chapter describes how trustees can become involved in monitoring and assessing the curriculum. Although the central responsibilities for making curricular and academic personnel decisions clearly rest with the faculty and the academic administration, the board's role is not passive. If informed questions are put in the right way to the right people at the right time, in the context of evaluating strategic commitments, the monitoring process is potent and belongs at the center of the board's responsibilities.

DATA POINT

63% of respondents said their boards had discussed adding new academic programs in the last five years. **78%** on the public side said they discussed new programs, **58%** on the private side.

The academic programs of American colleges and universities are increasingly complex and typically include a variety of curricular offerings serving diverse objectives. The largest universities offer degrees, certificates, and programs that include virtually every known discipline and field of professional study, at every level from the associate degree to the doctorate. Undergraduate degrees may be offered in 100 or more disciplinary fields and interdisciplinary programs, with graduate programs at various levels approaching the same number. Even small institutions reflect this complexity, as new programs constantly are developed in response to new curricular trends and market opportunities.

Trustees can understand the basic structure of academic programs because there is an inner logic to many of the courses and learning experiences in the overall curriculum. The offerings of an academic department or program can be examined through a lens that focuses on their crosscutting purposes and connections. Taking this into account, the board can monitor and evaluate how the offerings of the various departments and schools serve general education, undergraduate majors, interdisciplinary studies, professional education, and graduate programs. So, in addition to considering departmental offerings in terms of the internal logic of the disciplines, the board can analyze them strategically. The emphasis then shifts to analyzing how a course helps the institution meet the objectives of its various degree types, levels, and programs.

Other central dimensions of the educational purposes of colleges and universities are important to examine as well. Among them are strategic issues related to research, as well as the ways campus-life programs and experiences foster the personal and intellectual development of students. Boards also will need to examine the centrality of enrollment planning and management as the mechanisms that underwrite the strategic coherence and logic of the institution's academic offerings.

The final sections of this chapter focus on the evaluation of academic programs through a discussion of assessment, program review, and accreditation. These topics have been at the heart of public-policy deliberations about higher education for the past two decades. Governing boards need to be involved in the discussions about assessment and consider its implications for their own institutions.

General Education

The place to begin thinking strategically about the academic program is general education. In this distinctly American approach, virtually every associate or baccalaureate degree must include requirements (often mandated by accreditation standards) for study in diverse academic fields outside of the student's intended major. In most parts of the world, by contrast, university students focus immediately on their major field of interest, including those who study law and medicine. Usually, about half of a student's program is composed of general education courses, which carry many of the goals that institutions establish in their mission statements. On most campuses, general education represents a substantial investment of institutional resources, especially in the arts and sciences.[1]

Evolving concepts of general education provide an important strategic window into the history of higher education in America. In the colonial period, a fixed classical course of studies was standard, so general education was collegiate education. At the end of the 19th century, the specialized disciplines began to gain centrality in the curriculum, and by the middle decades of the 20th century there were strong trends to fold all of collegiate study into free electives and a student's chosen disciplinary major. During the post-World War II era, the pattern of combining studies in breadth (general education) and depth (the major) became the norm. This approach has prevailed ever since.

But the universality of the prevailing broad categories of breadth and depth masks constant ferment about the meaning and purpose of general education. By the late 1960s and early 1970s, many institutions had sharply reduced or eliminated general education requirements. During this heady period of social change, students and faculty activists complained of the "irrelevance" of such courses to real life and of the heavy hand of requirements that failed to motivate students. The first critiques of the blindness of the curriculum to issues of race, gender, and ethnicity also were part of the period's deconstruction of general education. Yet within a decade, educators and other voices in society began to call for a return to a structured general education program. In recent decades, especially during the 1980s, a continuing process of curricular study and reform has touched nearly every college and university.

During this period of change, many institutions questioned the prevailing model for organizing general education around the fulfillment of "distribution requirements." As is well known, the standard model groups courses to meet requirements under broad classifications of related fields and disciplines such as the humanities and arts, the social sciences, the natural sciences, and mathematics. Reformers have found this approach unsatisfactory on many counts. As fields and disciplines have evolved, the formal classification of any given course under such a broad category as the "humanities" means less and less. So, for example, a course in logic is made equivalent to a course in the history of philosophy in meeting the humanities requirement because both courses happen to be from the same department. In fact, the patterns of reasoning and problem solving in logic may be much closer to the skills developed in a computer-science course classified as science or mathematics.

As this and countless other examples reveal, the problem is a failure to develop and articulate a compelling rationale for the student's selection of courses. The process is reduced to a search for courses that match a scheme without coherence or transparency. As students try simply to "get the requirement out of the way," they miss the opportunity to become conscious of the themes, issues, and methods that provide connections in their studies. Lacking a clear rationale, general education may fail to build the curiosity and motivation that emerge from a more purposeful experience.

Other failures of the standard model include the use of undifferentiated types of courses to serve the purposes of general education. There are often no criteria that make a given course a good candidate to serve as the student's initial or perhaps only involvement in a given field. So, one finds survey courses, introductions to disciplinary methods, specialized topics, and sometimes courses required of majors all on the long list of possible choices. Equally significant, teaching methods are as various as the courses, ranging from lecture courses to seminars. Nor are there always common emphases on pedagogies that involve students in speaking, reading original texts, completing extensive writing assignments, or being involved in collaborative learning projects.

General education reform has taken several directions. One pattern has developed programs that feature one or more core courses that all students take as part of a sequential program of studies. Frequently, faculty from different fields teach the core courses, so they can address common themes that cross disciplines. Although few institutions have developed an entire series of core courses for all of general education, many have developed a one-year or two-year humanities sequence required of all students.

Another common general education pattern has been the development of explicit criteria that define a limited number of courses designed to fulfill the goals of general education. The criteria can define both the intellectual focus of general education as well as the characteristic types of pedagogies to be emphasized. Commonly, faculties use "method of inquiry" as an emphasis to group general education courses, developing such categories as historical inquiry, social analysis, literary analysis, symbolic reasoning, and so on, as the organizing themes. With appropriate justification, courses from different departments may satisfy the criteria developed to define the method of inquiry. Thus, a religion course called the "History of Israel" may be a historical analysis course. Using our prior example, a logic course would be a course called "Symbolic Reasoning," as would calculus or a course on computer languages.

As to methods of teaching, common criteria for general education often are developed, emphasizing writing, oral performance, collaborative learning, and the use of original works, as opposed to textbooks.

When an effective rationale for general education has been developed, it assists students in becoming deliberate—conscious of the knowledge, skills, and abilities they are developing through their studies. They can make more purposeful choices among courses, addressing strengths they seek to bolster or taking courses to improve on a weakness. (Some of the evolving efforts to develop more coherent programs of general education parallel similar efforts regarding academic majors and other components and levels of the total curriculum.)

An articulation of the goals of general education also produces important reference points for the assessment of effectiveness. Increasingly, colleges and universities are defining areas in which student capacities, skills, competencies, and values should be developed through general, liberal, and professional education. These include effective communication (writing, speaking, and reading), quantitative reasoning, computer use, problem solving, critical and integrative thinking, cross-cultural awareness, and civic responsibility. When these objectives are singled out, students can be assessed consistently and can assess themselves. They also can more easily relate their education to other contexts in personal, professional, and civic life.

How Trustees Can Monitor the General Education Program

General education programs are of great strategic significance to an institution. They may bear the stamp of an institution's identity and embody some of its distinctive capabilities. They consume substantial resources and occupy much of a student's time in the early college years. A large body of research confirms that a student's persistence in college is closely related to meaningful academic involvement and successful relationships with peers and faculty formed early in the college years. Students who are underprepared for college work are especially vulnerable in general education programs, because they are required to take courses in a large variety of fields and are exposed to challenges in areas where they may be particularly weak. The commitment of resources is significant in such areas as faculty advising and academic-skills development programs.

As trustees monitor general education programs, they may ask the following questions:
- How long has the current general education program been in effect, and when was it last reviewed?
- Does the general education program provide a competitive advantage in attracting and retaining capable students?
- What is the rationale for general education requirements, and do they constitute a coherent program of study?
- What proportion of a student's total program is committed to general education?
- What are the criteria for general education courses, both as to intellectual content and pedagogy?
- How does the institution assess the effectiveness of general education?
- What resource and staffing issues have arisen in general education?
- How are the institution's defining strengths and characteristics incorporated into the general education program?

Academic Majors

If general education provides the breadth for undergraduate study, then the academic major supplies the depth. Majors typically are focused in an academic department or, in a large institution, in professional schools such as those for business, engineering, or education.

As disciplinary specialties have increasingly defined intellectual life, their imprint on the curriculum has become dominant. Many faculty readily acknowledge that a continuing process of specialization within fields and subfields has led to a proliferation of courses in their own departments. Over time, many departments have become loose confederations of proponents of different methods and specialties linked by a common subject matter and shared professional self-awareness. So, for example, the quantitative political scientist who studies voting trends using complex computer models may have very little in common with the Plato expert across the hall whose specialty is ancient political theory.

As a consequence of these professional disparities, departments crafting the requirements for a major frequently have difficulty establishing intellectual coherence and an evident rationale. In the worst cases, students simply are required to take eight to ten courses from a long list of possibilities; hence, there is no sequencing in the course selection patterns, no definition of essential skills and methodologies, and no differentiation of core subject matters. Although many departments provide upper level experiences and seminars that bring coherence to the major, many others lack the inclination or resources to provide such integration. From a strategic point of view, there are many lost opportunities to connect the work within an academic major to the institution's stated educational goals.

At most institutions, the need to create closer connections between the breadth and depth dimensions of the student's experience is significant. As institutions have become more intentional regarding the purposes of a liberal education—often defining a powerful set of intellectual capacities as its results—the program in general education usually carries the burden of attaining the goals. Departments often are silent or diffident about objectives for the major, perhaps because fostering knowledge about the methods and the content of the discipline is the obvious purpose. Yet from the perspective of the institution's ability to define itself strategically, there is a ready advantage in reflecting coherently about the impact of the total educational experience on the student.

DATA POINT

37% of respondents said revising the general education curriculum in light of current thinking about students' educational needs is very important. In 1984, this percentage was **24%**. In 2001, **12%** called it unimportant, compared with **28%** in 1984.

In examining majors and departments, trustees will want to consider the following questions:

- Have departments developed a coherent rationale for their majors that defines a logical order of requirements and course sequences?
- How do the goals of the major relate to the institution's goals in general education?
- How do programs and departments assess their effectiveness in reaching their goals for student learning?
- Which departments have developed an external reputation for distinctive strengths and achievements, perhaps in preparing students for graduate study, in developing innovative teaching strategies, or in providing leadership in the discipline?
- What have been the enrollment patterns of student majors and minors in various

departments over the past ten years?

- What are the enrollment patterns among students who are taking departmental courses either as electives or as general education requirements?
- How does the department handle proliferation of specialized courses in which there may be very low student enrollment?

Professional Studies

Current estimates are that 70 percent of undergraduates major in a professional field rather than in the arts and sciences. For many liberal arts institutions this fact, a result of a 30-year trend, raises strategic questions about how to allocate resources and represent the institution to the public. Among the many important educational issues is how to integrate professional and liberal arts majors.

Just as arts and sciences disciplines have multiplied their specialties, so have most professional fields continued to add new subject areas. One of the major pressures for larger numbers of courses and requirements comes from the specialized accrediting bodies that oversee and evaluate every professional program a campus offers. Specialized accreditors reflect the views of practitioners and of the professional professoriate about what new studies have become essential. At the same time, most accrediting bodies also emphasize the need for students to be competent in areas of general and liberal education.

A number of recurrent educational and strategic issues arise from these trends and realities. Educators in professional programs constantly are challenged to respond to the new requirements and expectations of the profession while maintaining a commitment to general education. Students in many professional fields, engineering being the classic example, encounter a tightly defined curriculum that allows little flexibility. As pressures have continued to intensify to add courses and increase requirements, many fields have become *de facto* five-year programs. Scheduling conflicts and resource limitations make it impossible in practical terms for students to meet all requirements in four years.

As part of this process, general education for professional students often is squeezed to a minimum, and professional schools sometimes introduce their own basic requirements in such areas as statistics. From the perspective of the central administration, the proliferation of specialized requirements is a principal frustration, because it represents duplication of effort, fragmentation of education, and inefficient use of resources. At an educational level, these trends testify to the overspecialization of knowledge and the widening distances among different professional fields. In most institutions, increased cooperation between professional and liberal education is a major strategic opportunity and necessity—educationally and financially.

Trustees will want to pose a variety of questions, most with a clear strategic orientation:

- What have been the trends in enrollment in the professional fields over the past ten years?
- Do any of the undergraduate professional programs take more than four years to complete? Why?
- How do the themes and emphases of programs in general and liberal education connect

with the emphases and objectives in professional fields?

- How does the institution gather information from practitioners and theorists about emerging needs in the professions and about the institution's responsiveness to important trends?
- What is the pattern of professional students in securing employment and in job performance?
- Are there good examples of cooperation and program integration between and among professional fields and the arts and sciences?
- What is the experience of the professional programs in relationship to specialized accrediting bodies, and what are the results of the evaluations?
- What are the results of the internal assessment of professional programs?
- Has the university attained special recognition for its achievements in its professional fields?
- Is it possible for students who are majoring in one field or discipline to enroll in another professional field as a minor or as a double major, perhaps by extending the length of study or completing courses during the summer?

Interdisciplinary Studies

As the various academic disciplines have concentrated more intently on tightly bounded specialties, a countervailing response has been a focus on broader problems that require multiple forms of analysis to be understood. As is often noted, the complex processes of living systems and human societies are inherently interwoven and interactive. They do not simplify and unbundle themselves for the convenience of disciplines. To be responsive to changing intellectual and social trends, faculty and administrators regularly propose new interdisciplinary programs to the governing board. Research institutions create "institutes" and "centers," defined around interdisciplinary research agendas that focus on everything from issues in applied technology to the analysis of pressing social problems. In many cases, these institutes or centers also sponsor undergraduate or graduate degree programs or offer integrated courses of study sometimes called "concentrations" or, more traditionally, "minors." A typical large university has literally dozens of interdisciplinary programs and centers that attract a variety of sponsors and donors, often in partnership with other universities or with government or industry.

At the undergraduate level, there are parallel strategic developments, although typically the primary emphasis is on teaching and the creation of interdisciplinary majors. There are many motivations for such programs. Institutions are able to enrich and enlarge the program choices available to students by combining courses and experiences to address common problems that transcend disciplinary boundaries. The result may be both a competitive advantage and an intellectual strength. In some cases, the methods and literature of interdisciplinary fields have become so stable and widespread that standard new fields of inquiry have been created. So, for example, biochemistry and molecular biology together have become a discrete field. In other cases, a program of studies may be more clearly cross-disciplinary or multidisciplinary, as quite different methods and subjects are drawn together to focus on a common phenomenon, such as American Studies or Urban Studies. Many of the newer endeavors to enlarge the diversity of the curriculum also have led to the creation of interdisciplinary programs. Both Women's Studies and African-American Studies, now joined by a large variety of other programs that focus on distinctive ethnic experiences and cultures, represent ways to bring together recent research from various fields and disciplines.

DATA POINT

54% of respondents said developing new academic programs in response to changing internal demand is very important. **67%** from public institutions give this response, **51%** from privates.

With regard to the use of resources, interdisciplinary programs present both ingenious designs as well as taxing problems. Usually, most of the courses a student will take in an interdisciplinary program already exist within the offerings of a department. To organize these into a coherent program of study is a highly cost-effective way of deploying a university's resources. At the same time, once a program is created, it quickly develops a self-interest. Because various departments control the basic resources of the program—faculty time—there is always the anxiety that changes in faculty personnel will remove essential resources from the program. Moreover, integrative seminars or courses that require new resources often are necessary to complement the existing departmental offerings. As a consequence of these factors, most institutions are involved in continuing discussions and debates about whether programs should evolve into separate units or departments with full control over their destinies or, alternatively, whether structure as a program is the appropriate form of organization.

Along with the debates over organization come continuing discussions and disagreements about the intellectual validity of many interdisciplinary enterprises. Many faculty members discount interdisciplinary programs as loose confederations of methods and subjects lacking the depth and coherence of a disciplinary major. The contrary view, equally well represented, is that interdisciplinary programs provide students with intellectual capacities and understandings that represent the most important possibilities of liberal education. Students are taught to see relationships in knowledge and to use different methods to address common intellectual or social problems. These integrative capacities are seen as precisely the talents that are needed in civic and professional contexts throughout life.

Trustees will want to ask many of the same questions about interdisciplinary programs as were suggested to monitor general education and the academic major. In addition, trustees might consider the following:

- Have interdisciplinary programs become an important part of the academic program as indicated by their number and by student enrollment?
- How do interdisciplinary programs relate to the mission and strategic identity of the institution? Do they represent a competitive advantage?
- What criteria have to be satisfied regarding faculty capabilities and student interests before a program can be established?

- What funding mechanisms support programs, centers, and institutes?
- What are the financial and quality criteria for a program to be discontinued?

Graduate Programs

The noted diversity of American colleges and universities is nowhere more evident than in the enormous variety and range of programs they offer at the graduate level. At one end of the spectrum are hundreds of institutions that offer no graduate work, and at the other are universities with thousands of graduate students in dozens of master's and doctoral programs in every sphere of academic endeavor.

Mission statements frequently offer little predictability as to what graduate-level programs an institution offers and why. Sometimes historical circumstances alone explain the existence of a graduate degree, because it may not be part of a wider pattern of programs. Graduate offerings also may appear as part of an institution's efforts to enlarge the scope of its mission and to aspire toward status as a major university; this was a common thrust as regional institutions and former teacher's colleges expanded their ambitions throughout the 1960s and 1970s. Or it may be that the professional interests of faculty members with strong research commitments are part of the justification for introducing new master's and doctoral programs, reflecting the intimate ties between graduate programs and research productivity.

The sobering financial realities of the last 20 years, with cycles of boom and bust in state financing, have created substantial resistance to new graduate programs from many quarters. Legislators have pressed state coordinating boards and campus administrations to justify every new proposal and eliminate redundant programs. In state systems, every institution is required to avoid duplication of programs that are readily available in the same educational market.

The dynamics of graduate education in the arts and sciences raise strategic issues of focus, excellence, and effective use of resources. In institutions with a large number of successful doctoral programs, there should be synergy among faculty research, graduate student involvement in research, teaching assistantships, and funding sources (often through sponsored research). These elements should hold together as an economic and educational whole. Trustees should know if the synergy is lacking. The central *fiscal* reality is that the great majority of graduate students in arts and sciences generally enroll in doctoral study only with substantial fellowship support and/or with teaching assistantships. If an institution lacks endowment income, grants, research income, or state funding to support the fellowship awards, then the cost of the subsidy for graduate education is borne by general tuition revenue, most of which is paid by undergraduates.

Even the wealthiest, world-class research universities have had to focus their graduate offerings and to reduce the size of their enrollments to keep a strategic balance in their programs. Not every department can offer a doctorate in every specialty or subspecialty. Some departments may be able to aspire to comprehensive excellence, but most others will need to limit their leadership to a few areas. Many doctoral institutions that lack excellent resources or established reputations will take the approach of offering doctorates only in some departments, using the criterion of selective excellence in a different way.

Graduate programs in professional fields or at the master's level not leading to a doctorate raise a different set of strategic issues. In professional fields such as law or business, most students do not condition attendance on fellowship aid, nor is there a tradition of having students carry part of the undergraduate teaching responsibility. As a result, graduate professional programs do not draw as heavily from central resources and typically are expected to generate their own income. From a strategic perspective, the central question for many graduate professional programs is their relationship to other programs and disciplines of the university. In what ways can they cooperate with other programs and departments to strengthen the intellectual life of the whole institution?

Master's programs represent other strategic issues and opportunities, some of which relate to responsiveness to regional needs for continuing professional development. For example, thousands of K-12 teachers are enrolled in master's programs, representing an important form of university service in the improvement of education. If a university has chosen service to local and regional professions as a strategic aim, then it will be ready to develop master's programs to serve relevant professional groups. If existing fixed costs—classrooms, laboratories, and current faculty—can be used to advantage, then the programs may produce net revenue. If they do not pay for themselves, warning flags should rise among the administration and the board, because the costs may represent a drain of resources away from higher priorities.

Board review of graduate programs will draw a variety of questions, many echoing those suggested for other programs. In addition, trustees will want to know the following:

- What is the strategic focus of the graduate program in general and of each particular program?
- What is the relationship of each graduate program to the mission of the institution?
- Does the program duplicate others that are readily available in the same market?
- Do the numbers show the program to require a subsidy, or is it self-sufficient?
- What does the program contribute to the institution's research or public service mission?

Research

Research is not a specific course of study, but there is no doubt about its strategic centrality in the mission of most universities and many colleges. In general, American universities have a splendid record in research that sets the standard for the world in many fields. Faculty members see the creation of knowledge as a defining characteristic of the academic profession. In America and around the world, the quality of an individual's or an institution's research typically defines academic quality and prestige. Where questions arise is in the precise strategic role of research in each institution and for each faculty member.

The issue is usually settled at the two ends of the institutional spectrum, as defined by level of study. In institutions with large graduate and doctoral programs, the central importance of the research mission is a given. In two-year institutions, faculty are not expected to conduct research. In the middle are institutions with a mixture of undergraduate and graduate programs, among which expectations for research, as a later chapter will discuss, vary enormously.

In this context, the strategic question is the central one. Without a clear and consistent sense of the role of research in the institution's mission and in its strategic goals, there will be a continuing ambiguity that may lead to missed opportunities, frustration and conflict, or wasted resources.

One of the first distinctions for board members to consider is the difference between sponsored and unsponsored research, both of which occur on virtually every campus. Beyond its intrinsic educational value, research has a muscular presence in institutions with large graduate programs because it has become a central mechanism for funding the whole enterprise. Grants from corporations, some foundations, and especially from government sources bring large payments of overhead to compensate the institution for the use of its facilities and the indirect costs involved in supporting sponsored research. With overhead rates of anywhere from 10 percent to more than 75 percent of the amount of the grant, it is obvious that a multimillion-dollar research grant produces large sums to underwrite university expenses.

Over time, most research-oriented institutions have come to depend on overhead and related grant income as a staple of their budgets, so the strategic financial reasons to emphasize research are not hard to understand. Trustees should be aware of their institution's research overhead policies and practices, trends in sponsored research, and the impact of grants on the university's fixed and variable costs, especially because these issues can become matters of political and public scrutiny.

Increasingly, corporations in scientific and technological fields are developing research partnerships with universities or with entities controlled by universities. In some cases, these joint ventures have the potential to provide lucrative revenues from copyrights and stock in start-up companies. Each venture needs to be scrutinized in terms of the key issues of intellectual property rights and the provisions of the contract over time, as well as centrality to mission. Each cooperative arrangement will raise specific questions about the university's academic autonomy. Are the university's values compromised if there are restraints on the free circulation of research results because of the proprietary interests of the sponsoring corporation? This fundamental strategic question is also at the heart of academic professional ethics, so it merits continuing board review.

Among institutions or in departments in which there is little sponsored research, different strategic questions arise. Without income from sponsorship, who pays for the research time of the faculty? If it is student tuition, which principle justifies the expenditure? Unfunded research may well be justified by a variety of strategic factors, including the quality and reputation of the institution, its programs, and faculty. Published research undergirds the quality of a faculty member's work, while sustaining effectiveness in teaching. Yet hard questions have to be raised at a certain point in the strategic analysis of unsponsored research. The drive of some faculty for more time to conduct their research finally has to be viewed against the institution's mission and be measured against other commitments, including teaching and service to the institution. Academic administrators must continually analyze research costs in the form of faculty time, and the board can play an important role in periodically reviewing these issues and raising its own questions.

DATA POINT

10% of respondents said changing faculty work-load policies to encourage more research and publication is very important. **53%** said it is not important. **65%** from doctoral institutions, **40%** from master's, and **45%** from baccalaureates called it moderately or very important.

- What is the role of research as defined by the institution's mission and strategic plan?

- What types of sponsored research are taking place in the institution? Who are the major sponsors? What are the funding patterns, overhead rates, budgetary consequences, and other financial considerations, both now and in the future?

- Does the institution have clear policies regarding intellectual property rights and the publication of results of research sponsored by corporations? Have they been recommended by an appropriate faculty body, reviewed by legal counsel, and considered by the board?

- What are the institution's policies for unsponsored research? What is the strategic role of such research? Is the faculty teaching load defined in terms of expectations for research and publication? Can released time be awarded to faculty who are completing publications or research projects?

Student Development

Student learning that occurs outside the classroom has long been considered an important part of higher education. During the past several decades, a variety of research has testified to the importance of the total campus experience in contributing to a student's personal and intellectual development.[2] To the extent that education develops fundamental human powers, the entire range of resources and activities available to students in a community of learning become significant. Trustees should be knowledgeable about this dimension of their institution's educational program.

In particular, students who have a residential campus experience are afforded opportunities for growth and learning in many contexts. Most campuses have developed a rich repertoire of events in the performing and visual arts, as well as a variety of lectures and programs that bring prominent visitors to the campus from all walks of life. Sometimes related to course offerings themselves, these programs extend and enliven the lessons of the classroom. They contribute to enlarging the intellectual interests and curiosity of students and create a stimulating campus environment.

Campuses also offer students an enormous menu of opportunities to participate in intercollegiate or intramural athletics, student government, and other activities. In recent years, virtually every college and university also has created opportunities for students to become involved in volunteer service. Organizations such as Campus Compact and the Campus

Outreach Opportunity League (COOL) have encouraged service and stimulated links to the curriculum through various forms of service learning.

In all these ways, students have the opportunity to develop a range of personal capacities to become more self-aware, better organized and disciplined, and more effective both as leaders and members of a group. In relating to one another in various contexts, especially to people from different backgrounds, students strengthen their commitments to democratic decision-making processes and to such values as tolerance and respect. Ultimately, civic responsibility—a perennial goal of education—must take root in commitments and actions for it to be more than abstract theory.

The development of the many facets of student campus life into a powerful educational whole is not a matter of chance but of careful reflection and planning. The effort to connect the classroom with the educational possibilities of campus life is a never-completed task. It must address the challenge of everything that disrupts the priority of educational values, such as student abuse of alcohol or academic dishonesty. The goal is to build a powerful and inclusive community of learning. When based on a holistic educational philosophy and translated into creative campus programs, the total development of the student becomes a significant strategic opportunity and point of differentiation for the institution.

Trustees will want to raise questions such as the following as they review the sphere of student development:

- Has the institution articulated a coherent philosophy of student development that integrates curricular and cocurricular experiences?
- How has that philosophy been translated into explicit goals and related programs?
- How are the goals and programs evaluated?
- What is the nature and extent of student participation in volunteer service and in service learning?
- How effective are the institution's programs related to such issues as alcohol abuse, academic dishonesty, sexual aggression, and campus safety?
- How do the residential-life and athletic programs contribute to student learning and to the institution's educational purposes?

Enrollment Planning and Management

The purposes, capacities, and characteristics of an institution's students decisively shape its strategic identity. A fundamental condition for institutional and academic effectiveness is the alignment of an institution's academic programs with students' interests and abilities. For virtually every institution, the interplay between these central elements creates a continuing and central strategic challenge.

The most pressing challenge, especially for private colleges and universities, is to enroll consistently an adequate number of students to support existing programs and overhead. When institutions experience declining enrollments and high attrition, there usually is a serious strategic misalignment. The problem may be in a mismatch between the institution's academic programs and its potential student clientele, in poor public communication, weak recruitment efforts, or in difficulties related to the campus environment. Whatever the reason, institutions cannot fulfill their academic purposes and achieve their strategic goals until their enrollments are stable.

Even institutions that are in basic control of the size of their student body face varying strategic challenges in the enrollment arena. Many institutions have wide variations in enrollments among disciplines and schools, experience high attrition in some or many fields, lack the diversity they desire, or enroll a large number of undermotivated or underprepared students. Less obviously, but commonly, institutions offer general education programs or academic majors that do not take into account the specific characteristics of the student body or reflect particular institutional strengths. For example, many institutions with low selectivity and students of average ability insist on seeing themselves as educating an intellectual elite. Their programs may represent a mismatch with the real needs of their actual students. Trustees have a particularly significant role in questioning and assessing the way the institution aligns its enrollment-management plan with its resources, programs, and mission.

To deal with the centrality and complexity of enrollment issues, many institutions have created a high-level administrative position to take responsibility for enrollment planning. Included with the responsibility are admissions, retention, and (usually) the policy dimensions of financial aid. Whether a defined responsibility or not, the issue of admissions and enrollment should be close to the center of final responsibility in most institutions. Presidents and boards must be aware of the enormous leverage of the issues for virtually every financial, academic, and strategic goal of the institution.

Most institutions have developed enrollment models and marketing plans that reflect the strategic centrality of student characteristics and enrollment in realizing the institution's academic purposes. Most institutions' models are complex because of the many variables in the attendance patterns of today's students. On a national scale, students pursue their educations recurrently, transfer between institutions frequently, and study off campus, online, or abroad increasingly. An effective enrollment model captures the complex variety of institution-specific enrollment patterns. It allows the institution to project likely consequences of variations in enrollment related to policy changes in financial aid, housing policies, or programs.

Boards must closely follow student-enrollment issues because they are tied so intimately to the institution's academic identity and economic stability. In addition to questions raised in other sections, trustees will want to know the following:

• What is the institution's admissions

DATA POINT

89% of respondents from public institutions said it is important to change admission standards to alter the composition of their student bodies; **54%** from private institutions agreed. In 1984, **40%** of all institutions called this important; in 2001, **60%**.

profile over a ten-year period? The profile should include (1) the number of inquiries; (2) the percentage of inquiries that become applications; (3) the number of applications; (4) the percentage and number of accepted applicants; (5) the percentage (yield) of accepted applicants who matriculate; (6) the percentage of students who apply and who are accepted for early decision; (7) the high school rank, school background, and test scores (mean and median) of the entering class; and (8) the geographic, ethnic, and international backgrounds of the students.

- Which indicators in the institution's admissions profile have the greatest strategic significance for the institution?
- What are the central components in the institution's enrollment model? This should reflect both departing and returning students, in-state and out-of-state students, entering students, withdrawals, transfers, suspensions, leaves of absence, study abroad, and graduating seniors.
- What policy variables (such as student-aid policy) can the model use to make projections?
- How successful has the enrollment model been in projecting actual enrollment over a five-year period?

Assessment

Assessing educational quality has moved to the center of public-policy discussions of higher education. The immense popularity of "ranking" institutions in popular magazines and guides is one token of the deeply rooted American desire to know who is "best," preferably through quantified measures of quality. Some legislators and public officials believe that to receive a degree all students should be required to take a "high-stakes test." They seek some sort of measurement that ostensibly would allow direct comparisons and ratings of institutions and programs as a way to ensure that funding follows quality.[3] Behind these proposals is the desire to be assured that the public's expenditure of funds is producing worthwhile results.

Most presidents, provosts, deans, and faculty members shudder at the more extreme suggestions. They are keenly aware of the enormous variation in admissions standards at different types of institutions, the dramatic differences in institutional missions, varying conceptions of the best pedagogies, and contrasting interpretations of a discipline even in the same department. Probably no two students ever study exactly the same courses in

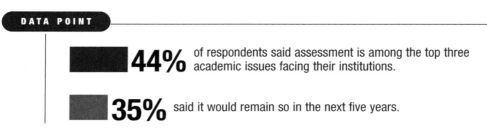

DATA POINT

44% of respondents said assessment is among the top three academic issues facing their institutions.

35% said it would remain so in the next five years.

completing a degree. How universal ratings of quality might ever be constructed is bewildering to most educators.

If *how* one might develop standard tests or measures of quality boggles the mind, *what* one might measure is equally perplexing. The mission statement of every college and university offers exalted goals about the development of the human mind and spirit that are so deep, vague, and comprehensive as to defy scientific measurement. Should the mission state, as it often does, that a college's aim is to produce a love of learning or a sense of civic responsibility, it quickly becomes obvious that the serious, scientific measurement of these goals poses a staggering challenge. One never can know for sure what a student brings to the table, gains from other life experiences, or derives specifically from a college course or experience. To measure civic commitments, does one analyze a person's voting record, daily reading of the newspaper, participation in civic groups, actions taken to support equal opportunity? How does one know what these actions truly mean and what influenced them? As educators deal with these issues, it should be noted, they usually have far more exacting requirements for what counts as a valid and reliable assessment than do many of the critics who are seeking data about student learning.

Many of the discussions about assessment clearly involve people who hold different assumptions speaking past one another. In spite of this contention and confusion, most higher education institutions continue to make serious efforts to evaluate themselves. No longer do these institutions relate quality primarily to "inputs" (the size of the endowment, the credentials of the faculty, or the number of books in the library, for example), but rather to "educational outcomes"—to what students actually are learning. Most states, either through legislative action or the mandates of coordinating boards, have enacted requirements for institutional assessment. Every regional accrediting body, and most specialized ones, has requirements related to the evaluation of institutional effectiveness, including the educational achievement of students. Thus, it is safe to say that every college or university has developed procedures and protocols to address the issue of assessment.

As assessment has moved up the agenda of American higher education, it has followed a dominant pattern. Each institution has developed mechanisms to assess the particular ways it approaches the fulfillment of its mission. The typical approach is to use a range of information about performance and characteristics as a way of measuring the institution's ability to achieve its own goals. Much of the data collected and analyzed may be usefully compared with data from other institutions, so benchmarking is common. Yet because circumstances between institutions often are so dissimilar, comparisons are rarely seen as "ratings" or absolute, stand-alone indicators of educational quality. The primary goal is to glean insights from the information as a basis for improving processes.

Indeed, the corporate world's total-quality movement has had its effect on campuses. Although few institutions use the language and systematic methods of the total-quality system, especially in the academic sphere, the spirit of self-improvement through the analysis of information permeates higher education. When it works best, assessment is tied to the continuing work of strategic planning and budgeting and becomes internalized within the regular decision-making processes of the institution. It becomes part of a continuing effort to integrate the setting of goals with the assessment of results and leads to the translation of evaluations into ways to enhance programs and procedures.

Within this process, institutions can use a variety of information that is often imbedded in institutional life or that can be developed through new cycles of data gathering. The criteria as to what counts as good information in this kind of assessment can be relatively generous, since no one claims that the data represent absolute measures or that they pinpoint the causes of educational achievement. For example, much of the information campuses collect comes from interviews or questionnaires that record student opinions and evaluations. Even though the source is subjective, the data can be reliable and valid measures of opinion if good protocols are used. Student opinions in turn serve as indicators of whether educational goals are met. When students are asked whether they have developed commitments to democratic values, for example, their answers can be seen as proxies for that measure. If the responses paint a picture that seems out of step with expectations or with the results at benchmark colleges, then the institution has the ability to probe the question, pursue leads, search for explanations, and then perhaps change practices to achieve different results.

Most institutions have developed a significant number of indicators they issue in various forms, often in a publication called a "Fact Book." Some of the indicators address specific educational outcomes, while many of them represent measures that describe the institutional framework within which educational goals are to be met. So, for example, institutions invest a lot of time and energy developing comparative faculty salary data. To attract and retain faculty members who have the characteristics (terminal degrees, teaching skills, scholarly potential) the institution needs to reach its educational goals, it must offer competitive salaries and benefits. The data serve as a strategic indicator of the institution's intent to reach these goals.

What do contemporary institutions want to know about their academic programs? Trustees should seek assessment indicators on a regular basis that reflect patterns of educational achievement. The following are good examples of what a board might reasonably expect:

- Data on the retention of students from year to year and graduation rates within four, five, and six years.
- Data reflecting institutional assessments of student intellectual skills and competencies as developed in specific courses, especially in general education.
- Results of surveys of graduating students and of alumni five and ten years after graduation reporting on their achievements and judgments of satisfaction and of academic quality, compared with results from benchmark institutions.
- The results of departmental exit interviews and surveys indicating the quality of the student experience of the academic major.
- A survey of all graduates within the first year of graduation to assess admission to graduate and professional schools and patterns of employment.

- The results of student performance on any licensure tests or related professional examinations such as the C.P.A., bar examinations, and state teacher exams.
- The results of any examinations used by departments that participate in national testing programs in various fields and disciplines.
- The results of student performance on the Graduate Record Examination.
- The products of students who develop portfolios indicating their levels of competency and achievement.
- The results of national surveys and testing instruments that assess student engagement in learning or basic capacities for logical and critical thinking, problem solving, and effective communication.

The foregoing list represents a sampling of indicators that can be easily identified. Of greater importance is the way such summary data lead to follow-up studies of significant educational issues.

If an institution, for example, develops a new emphasis on "best practices" in active learning, logic dictates that it assess the new approaches. To do so, institutions can search for assessment studies or methods that already have been developed in national surveys. There are several benefits in seeking connections to ongoing national projects. One is that the cost of developing valid instruments, prohibitive for any one institution, has been borne by many others, including foundations. Second, national studies may provide useful benchmark data that suggest areas of relative strength and weakness.

As institutions pursue the leads that performance indicators provide, they should consistently press for the strategic significance of what they are learning about themselves. What stands out against the competition? What seem to be unanticipated results? Where do we seem to have higher or lower patterns of achievement than the profile of our students might predict? Trustees have a special vantage point from which to pose these questions.

Beyond the possibilities for strategic assessment lie opportunities for self-evaluation that are imbedded in the institution's own standard data about itself. Patterns of course selection, when seen as parts of a long trend line, are worth careful scrutiny. When departments undertake this kind of work, they often are surprised that 60 percent to 70 percent of their enrollment is limited to a handful of courses, while a large number of upper division offerings have marginal class sizes. Studies of student transcripts also can provide rich data to support inquiries related to general education, the use of electives, and patterns in the major.

Finally, trustees should be made aware of the kinds of evaluations of student learning that are part and parcel of individual courses. There is every reason to believe that student learning is being effectively fostered and assessed in courses that require a lot of writing, class presentations, graded participation, and essay exams. The criteria for grading can be related easily to demonstrated skills, capacities, and knowledge. Student work of this kind also is available to be scrutinized by others, including peers from other campuses. The credibility of the learning and grading associated with this kind of approach to student evaluation contrasts with that of courses in which multiple-choice tests are the basis for student grades.

Program Review

Most campuses, especially larger institutions, require periodic program reviews based on significant self-studies. Program reviews typically involve a panel of two or three experts from other institutions who visit the campus after a thorough review of the department's self-analysis. Carried out with care and commitment, the process of program review can bring substantial benefits, particularly as part of a continuing process of strategic planning.

There also are many dangers in program review, of course. Feuds or disagreements in departments often create heavy static in the process. Sometimes, both the department being analyzed and the outside reviewers can have a narrow vision, presuming that the main goal of the endeavor is to generate evidence to convince the administration to provide more resources to the department under review. With some orientation at the outset of the process, however, departments can focus on the larger concerns of the analysis of student learning and the strategic objectives of the institution. The key is to build the centrality of these concerns into the process and to expect, for example, that abundant samples of student work will be part of the self-study materials and that meetings with students will be prominent in the campus visit. With an increased emphasis on assessment and strategic thinking, program review becomes a promising aspect of the total process of institutional evaluation. It can become the point where the broad goals of an institution systematically connect with key departmental concerns.

Accreditation

As most trustees know, accreditation comes in two primary forms, institutional and specialized. The evaluation of the whole institution every ten years falls to one of six regional accrediting bodies spread geographically across the nation. Specialized accrediting groups, with somewhat different schedules, evaluate specific disciplinary or professional programs, sometimes including programs with a variety of subdisciplines, such as business.

Regional and specialized accreditation have much in common. They both represent a process of voluntary self-regulation through which the members of the accrediting organization assess one another based on standards and procedures approved by the member-

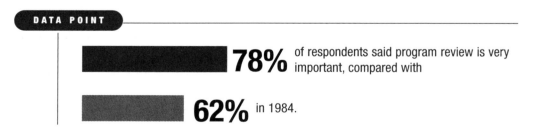

DATA POINT

78% of respondents said program review is very important, compared with

62% in 1984.

ship itself. Although interested in the process, the federal government is not involved in the assessment of individual institutions, except in the review of teacher-education programs. The distinctiveness of American self-regulation is in contrast with European and other higher education systems around the globe. In these systems, the national government often is a central player in quality-assurance reviews, even though the evaluation process usually also relies on peer assessments.

Another common set of characteristics has to do with the overall method or process by which accreditation occurs. Each accrediting body develops a set of criteria or standards, often requiring various forms of self-assessment, as the point of reference for a self-study by the institution or the specialized program. The next step is a visit to the campus by a team of peers to discuss the self-study report and interview members of the faculty, staff, student body, and trustees. Finally, the visiting committee develops a report that is submitted to campus leaders, as well as to the unit under review in cases of specialized accreditation.

That report and the campus response is the basis on which a review is made by a central peer committee of the accrediting body, after which a recommendation for final action is submitted to the accrediting organization's ultimate decision-making authority. The reaffirmation of accreditation often is accompanied by a request that certain issues of compliance be addressed in follow-up reports within a specified time. Serious problems may lead to sanctions, ranging from warning to probation to loss of membership.

One of the major differences between the regional and specialized accrediting processes is the largely mandatory nature of the former and the voluntary nature of the latter. Regional accreditation not only is a must to retain eligibility for many foundation and corporate grants, but also—and most vitally—for an institution's students to be eligible for federal loans and grants. The U.S. Department of Education has its own process for recognizing regional and other accrediting organizations, and students become eligible for federal support only if one of these recognized bodies accredits the institution.

Specialized accrediting bodies enjoy various degrees of influence, prestige, and visibility. Institutions participate in specialized accreditation primarily to maintain their reputation in the field and among employers. The one major exception to the voluntary character of specialized accreditation relates to the American Bar Association (ABA) and its accreditation process. Because only graduates of ABA-accredited law schools can sit for the bar exam in most states, accreditation is a practical necessity.

The accrediting process is criticized on many grounds, however. Many in government believe standards are far too low. Faculty and administration fear interference in the decision-making authority of the campus, or they believe that technical compliance with accrediting rules becomes an end in itself.

Nonetheless, there is little to be gained by magnifying the annoyances and problems of accreditation. It provides a basic set of expectations to protect the public from abuse. Whatever its weaknesses, it seems far superior to direct governmental regulation. Its goal should be to contribute to the institution's own efforts at self-improvement. Those who participate should get an early start on the process, experience it from the inside by participating in the reviews of other campuses, and look for ways the effort can produce benefits locally. Time and energy are far better spent anticipating issues and addressing them in advance than in filing endless reports at the conclusion of the process.

Trustees always are part of each regional accreditation self-study and visit, so they need to be aware of the broad issues and expectations of accreditation. They should receive an orientation as to the specific issues that the institution is likely to confront in the accreditation visit. They would do well to read sections of the self-study report relating to their committee responsibilities on the board, especially if they are to meet members of the visiting team. They also might review the results of the last accreditation visit. Trustees who appear to defer all decisions on every matter to the administration or who are poorly informed about the institution make a poor impression during the campus visit. Accreditation is a high-leverage process, so there is every reason for boards, as the institution's final authority, to monitor and contribute to its success. If the final report contains recommendations for changes or improvements or, more importantly, proposes specific sanctions, the board should ensure that these matters are raised to the top of the institution's agenda.

[1] For a brief account of many of the trends discussed in chapter three, see Schneider, Carol Geary, and Robert Shoenberg. *Contemporary Understandings of Liberal Education*. Washington, D.C.: Association of American Colleges and Universities, 1998. For an exhaustive analysis of these issues, see Gaff, Jerry G., and James L. Ratcliff, eds. *Handbook of the Undergraduate Curriculum: A Comprehensive Guide to Purposes, Structures, Practices, and Change*. San Francisco: Jossey-Bass Publishers, 1997.

[2] Among many possibilities, see Astin, Alexander W., *Four Critical Years: Effects of College on Beliefs, Attitudes, and Knowledge*. San Francisco: Jossey-Bass Publishers, 1977, and *What Matters in College? Four Critical Years Revisited*. San Francisco: Jossey-Bass Publishers, 1997. See as well, Kuh, George D., John J. Schuh, and Elizabeth J. Whitt. *Involving Colleges: Successful Approaches to Fostering Student Learning and Development Outside the Classroom*. San Francisco: Jossey-Bass Publishers, 1991.

[3] For a variety of perspectives on assessment see Part V, "Administration and Assessment of the Curriculum" in Gaff, Jerry G., and James L. Ratcliff, eds. *Handbook of the Undergraduate Curriculum: A Comprehensive Guide to Purposes, Structures, Practices, and Change*. San Francisco: Jossey-Bass Publishers, 1997.

CHAPTER 4

Strategic Analysis of the Academic Budget

The title of this chapter is something of a misnomer. Trustees will look long and hard, but without success, to find in university financial statements a single set of income and expense figures that constitute an "academic budget." Virtually all college and university budgets and audited statements divide the expenses associated with specific academic programs and activities into several broad categories, usually "Instruction," "Research," and "Academic Support" (basically libraries and technology). Even these categories are somewhat artificial, for Instruction includes many administrative expenses (supplies, telephone, copying, minor capital items, and travel) that support the work of academic departments. Additionally, one can argue that expenditures to support many things in academic institutions, including campus facilities, are educational expenses because they are essential to the delivery of the academic program. Yet expenditures to run academic facilities are included in "Operations and Maintenance."

The point is not to quibble over financial conventions and categories. Rather, it is to suggest that the academic budget is a concept more than a discrete set of numbers. As such, it can be used to identify a set of resources (library and technology), activities (teaching and research), and personnel (largely faculty) that directly support and implement academic programs. Thus, expenditures for academic programs and activities can be distinguished but not fully separated from other categories in the university budget. To make strategic decisions effectively, one must know the dynamics of the entire budget and understand the special characteristics of academic programs and personnel.

Trustees who work closely with budgets and financial statements in other contexts will quickly notice some of the special aspects of university and academic budgets. As with other service enterprises, such as hospitals and professional partnerships, the bulk of expenditures are for salaries and benefits. In most institutions, two-thirds to three-quarters of the total budget goes for personnel. Even in an area such as technology, the majority of continuing expenses are for people. In private institutions, expenditures for financial aid may range from 10 percent to 20 percent of the total budget. Not much is left for all other expenditures, such as books, equipment, and utilities.

Another singular characteristic of academic budgets is their high proportion of fixed costs. Tenured faculty positions represent permanent expenditures for salaries and benefits and constitute a large portion of the budget. Buildings must be maintained, heated, and lighted. Once the institution makes financial-aid commitments to students, it cannot renege. As a result, university budgets are strategically inflexible. Because of this, it is difficult to respond quickly to a financial problem. The first responses may be to freeze salaries and hiring and to make drastic cuts in such variable costs as travel and library purchases. Over the long term, institutions seek to restructure or rebalance costs in such pivotal areas as financial aid and administrative services. They also will seek to reduce or eliminate academic programs and positions.

The strategic challenge in cutting academic costs is to sustain the strength of the institution's core educational capacities, which are the very programs that attract and retain students and bring revenue from tuition. Small institutions in particular usually have the hardest time finding a way to deal with large budget reductions. Since they already operate with a limited range of offerings, cuts are likely to turn off prospective students. For these institutions, the long-term solution to financial challenges usually must include new revenues from increased enrollments, higher tuition, or larger donations.

Planning and Budgeting

Considered strategically, a college or university's budget should be read as the embodiment of the institution's identity and values. A well-informed and skilled analyst can unearth the institutional priorities and commitments that are embedded in financial data.

One of the decisive questions about every operating budget is whether strategic plans and priorities are driving the annual financial decision-making process. If strategic designs are to control the budget, then effective mechanisms must be in place to integrate planning and budgeting. Without effective processes of decision making and leadership—vested in an influential committee or in several individuals—operating budgets take on a life of their own and become disjointed puzzles reflecting political compromises or financial juggling acts. An important responsibility of trustees is to ensure that the means are in place to translate the academic commitments of strategic planning into the operating budget. The faculty and administration do the actual work of creating the budget, but the board's finance or budget committee reviews the process and the results. The board's academic affairs committee will be particularly sensitive to the implementation of academic priorities.

DATA POINT

55% of respondents said setting priorities for allocating resources to academic areas is very important. Among publics, **73%** called it very important; among privates, **50%.** In 1984, **59%** of publics and **57%** of privates rated this very important.

Committee leaders should consider such protocols as joint membership to ensure the implementation of academic priorities.

At many institutions, broad projections on financial issues of revenue and expense are first developed by the administration and then discussed with a budget committee composed of administrators and faculty members. With the outline of the budget in place, the committee deliberates on priorities in response to requests submitted by programs and departments. At this stage of the process, decisions must be consciously shaped by priorities in planning, or the coherence of the budget will be lost. It is worthwhile to devote time and energy in the committee to rehearse the larger strategic issues.

On most campuses, faculty involvement is a regular part of the budget process, though the weight of faculty recommendations is construed quite differently depending upon the institution and its traditions. Trustees will want to know the precise process that produces the budget, to ensure both fiscal discipline and the unity of academic planning and budgeting.

Uncontrollable events often seem to frustrate the connection between planning and budgeting in the academic sphere. Public institutions regularly must make rapid changes in their budgets, often at mid-year, as lean and rich funding cycles succeed one another with little warning. Strategic planning in such an environment is more than difficult, even with the best processes and procedures. Nonetheless, institutions in such circumstances can consider the planning and budgeting cycle as extending over a period of several years, with contingencies built into the process. Long-term goals and priorities are still essential, but they may have to be implemented over a longer planning horizon. Private institutions whose financial destinies are tied to variable enrollment also will want to develop flexible time periods to achieve their strategic goals.

Financial Models and Information Systems

College and university financial officers and outside experts have developed financial modeling capabilities to help with strategic and financial planning. These financial models can test plans to show the effect of varying assumptions about rates of increase or decrease in revenues and expenditures. By using an effective model, institutional officials can avoid huge frustrations in strategic planning.

Frequently, the planning process falls victim to an excess of enthusiasm for adding new academic programs and personnel, as well as the facilities to house them. Although blue-sky thinking is helpful in the early stages of planning, dreams and desires can outpace the institution's capacity to perform. As a result, the process can lose credibility, and subsequent rounds of planning will be much harder for people to take seriously. On the other hand, if planning has been closely tied to resource possibilities—even ambitious ones—the realization of goals over time creates a sense of confidence in the process. Because financial models may have long-range consequences and drive fundamental decisions, trustees will want to give both the process and its conclusions close scrutiny.

An effective information system pinpoints the leverage points of institutional and academic budgets and facilitates the periodic processes of strategic planning and financial modeling. Unless an institution knows the inner dynamic of its academic costs and how to control them, it is not in charge of its destiny.

Experienced financial officers and many presidents have an excellent sense of budgetary leverage points. They know, for example, how much revenue can be realized for each $100 increase in tuition, what each percentage increase in faculty and staff salaries means for total compensation costs, and how each percentage increase or reduction in unfunded financial aid influences net revenue. Trustees should expect this level of mastery within the administration. Insights of this kind can be translated into measures and ratios to be systematically tested in various runs of the financial model.

Another promising approach is the use of benchmarking information to make comparisons among similar institutions. Many institutions compare the percentage of their expenditures by budget category with those of other institutions. Although the comparisons sometimes may be awkward because of different expense classifications among institutions, wide variations from the mean nonetheless give an institution reason to study its spending patterns. Some institutions have joined consortia for the purpose of sharing data. Organizations such as the Consortium on Financing Higher Education (COFHE) and the Higher Education Data Service (HEDS) provide their members with continuing studies of institutional costs and characteristics, some of which have immediate relevance for the academic program. The studies use a variety of ratios, per-capita analyses, and trend lines to permit meaningful comparisons. Officials can find out, for example, why the same departments in comparable institutions differ so radically in cost. The raw data themselves will not provide a conclusive answer, but they suggest how the problem might be explored. Trustees will want to encourage such comparative studies.

Responsibility Center Budgeting

In large institutions that have multiple purposes and programs, budgeting often is done through "responsibility centers." In these cases, a school or a college becomes the budget center, rather than the general institution, and revenues and expenses are attributed or allocated to each unit. In a full-blown analysis, complete with accurate allocations of revenues and expenses for central administration (including such items as income from research overhead and financial aid and fellowships), it is possible to learn how much subsidy each unit requires or surplus income it produces. Institutions experienced with the system are able to assign large portions of their endowments to the various schools or departments, because gifts can be traced to their donor's original intent. Current grants and contracts also usually follow the pattern of award to a unit, and where that is not the case funds can be assigned to individual units by allocation formulas.[1]

Institutions use responsibility center budgeting with varying degrees of elaborateness. In some cases, the costs of different units are given much more focus than the revenue they may produce. Although the net revenue or deficit may be known for purposes of analysis, it may not be the basis for budgetary decision making. Decisions based on financial factors alone could cripple units that may be essential for educational reasons, such as those with low student enrollments. Many factors related to the quality and centrality of disciplines and their service to society also must be part of the decision-making equation. Nonetheless, by examining discrepancies in resource patterns between units, directions can be set over time to align their income and expenses. In sum, the financial and analytic work establishes a burden of proof, especially if trends indicate that a unit's financial position has deteriorated.

Although various dispersed patterns of budget decision making can produce powerful results, they also come with problems. True, putting budget decisions in closer proximity to academic decision makers creates an enterprising spirit that can unleash energy and creativity. Faculty and staff are much more likely to undertake new initiatives and seek new funds if they are aware that they will be the immediate beneficiaries of their success. But problems arise in responsibility center budgeting when the financial system is allowed to discourage efforts that reach across unrelated budgetary units. Then, the problem of territorialism, which is natural to the academic species under any circumstances, becomes intensified. Cooperative relationships and interdisciplinary opportunities may suffer. Artificial walls are built to reinforce natural barriers.

Small institutions also can benefit from the analysis of unit costs and revenues, even as they continue to operate with centralized budgets and decision-making authority. The exercise of relating revenue and expense by department or division can reveal results that have strategic significance. Perhaps officials will discover that a high-quality program depends heavily on the enrollment of students who need disproportionate amounts of financial aid. That discovery may translate into an effort to create special endowed scholarships funded through the next capital campaign.

Tuition Revenues and Financial Aid

As each institution develops a budgetary and financial information system appropriate to its size and complexity, the question of academic revenues, especially tuition income, is worth special consideration. It has taken on decisive strategic importance. Financial officers and many trustees have become especially conscious of the enormous financial leverage of programs of student financial aid and scholarships. Reflecting the serious challenges facing most families in financing a college education, government, private sources, and institutions themselves have dramatically increased financial aid to students since the late 1980s. All institutions now depend heavily on revenues generated by loans and grants awarded to students by federal and state programs alike.

In addition to awarding financial aid based on demonstrated need, virtually every institution itself provides an array of scholarships, usually based on achievement, to a large percentage of its students. In some institutions, the percentage can approach 90 percent. Much of the aid the institution awards is not backed by a revenue source, such as grants by donors or the government or by income from the endowment. Hence, the financial-aid "expenditure" actually is a tuition "discount," and accounting rules now require institutions to subtract such discounts from their revenues.

Every financial-information system, no matter how basic, should provide a specific indication of the amount and percentage of total tuition revenue that is discounted by unfunded student aid. When an institution reaches a high level of unfunded aid it cannot control, its future is in jeopardy. The situation reflects a weak market position for student enrollment and an inability to raise funds to replace the forgone student revenue. In proper balance, student aid can be a vital tool in recruiting a critical mass of capable, worthy, and needy students. Yet when discount rates exceed 40 percent to 50 percent of tuition revenue, alarm bells should be ringing throughout the institution. When such discount levels are reached, future tuition increases will net only a fraction of the income that would be produced at official, undiscounted rates. A vicious cycle of reduced income intensifies with each annual budget, reflecting the increasing proportion of students receiving large discounts as they move through their four-year course of study. All trustees should know precisely the institution's funded and unfunded discount rates as a percentage of tuition income, as well as the trends in these crucial indicators.

Containing Academic Costs

When the final budget study is complete, there should be no mysteries about what drives academic costs, especially in the instructional program. Salaries and benefits for faculty and staff members are always the largest share of the expense. If costs are to be contained or reduced in the academic area, then officials must find ways to offer the same program with fewer numbers of faculty or with a lower average salary and benefit package—or some means must be sought to reduce or eliminate parts of the program.

There are many ingenious and important ways to manage curricular programs to avoid wasting resources: streamlining departments that offer too many low-enrollment specialties, capping enrollments in some exploding fields that require additional faculty positions, curtailing or eliminating programs that no longer attract a critical mass of students, creating variable class sizes for courses that include large lecture courses. Yet the bottom line is that these possibilities and many similar ones will achieve little or no economies unless the institution employs fewer faculty or reduces the average cost of faculty compensation.

Most institutions use a variety of strategies to reduce the average cost of instruction. A typical pattern is to ensure that junior faculty with much lower salaries fill some of the positions vacated by senior people who retire or resign. These positions may not automatically return to the department but could be shifted to areas of higher priority or eliminated. Or an open position may be filled not by a tenure-track faculty member but by someone who holds a temporary, part-time, or adjunct appointment, which might end after a specific period. The difference in the cost per course between a highly compensated senior member of the faculty and a part-time professor is dramatic, when considered strictly as a financial question. (The problems and issues related to these trends will be considered in subsequent discussions of faculty personnel policies in Chapter 6.)

Many people continue to hope and expect that technology substantially will reduce instructional costs, but revolutionary breakthroughs have yet to occur. The Internet, e-mail, and desktop computers have restrained or reduced expenses for administrative support but not in amounts that approach the cost increases for technology itself. Because of these realities, trustees must be particularly aware when a new recurrent cost is added to an academic budget. For example, as faculty appointments initiated with grant funds ("soft money") come to an end, academic costs will grow if the positions are maintained in the regular operating budget.

DATA POINT

62% of respondents said their institutions discussed faculty compensation policies during the past five years. **22%** said the board set the policy. **50%** said the board was consulted, but the administration set the policy.

Keeping a sharp eye on the number of permanent positions is critical to academic budgeting, as is scrutiny of increasing recurrent costs that occur through salary increases and higher proportions of senior faculty.

The competitiveness of faculty salaries is a crucial strategic consideration to which most trustees are sensitive. Yet many institutions adopt strategic salary goals that they have not analyzed with requisite care and caution. The goals often are unrealistic and may never be realized, adding frustration to the problem. Because no dollars are more expensive than continuing salary dollars, it is crucial that salary goals and future resources be in close alignment. Salary improvements are vital strategic objectives, but they must be related to increases in permanent resources from tuition income, endowment campaigns, repeating annual gifts, or permanent state subsidies—or they must be tied to plans to reallocate resources from existing activities.

Given these considerations trustees will want to raise a variety of questions about the academic budget:

- By what mechanisms and procedures are the institution's strategic academic priorities translated into the operating budget?
- How effective is the financial model used in strategic planning in guiding budgets and other decisions about the use of resources?
- Does the institution use centralized or decentralized budgeting? What are the strengths and weaknesses of the current system?
- What methods does the institution use to analyze the relative costs of various academic programs and activities?
- How does the institution use benchmarking in its financial analyses? What has been learned from the process?
- Over the last three years, what specific steps have various academic units taken to constrain or reduce academic costs?
- How has the academic budget been able to accommodate areas, such as information technology, that have required large increases in expenditures?
- What long-range plans have been developed to restrain aggregate salary costs while providing competitive individual salaries?

- What checks are in place to control unplanned transitions of salaries from temporary funds to continuing funds?
- How many full-time faculty and staff are employed at the institution now, compared with three and five years ago?
- What are the funded and unfunded discount rates for scholarships and financial aid as a percentage of tuition revenue? What are the trends in these indicators?

[1] For a detailed discussion of the Stanford University Cost Model, see Rodas, Daniel J., et al. "Applying Contribution Margin Analysis in a Research University." In *Revitalizing Higher Education: Stanford Forum for Higher Education.* William F. Massy and Joel W. Meyerson, eds. Princeton: Peterson's Guides, 1995, pages 73-87.

CHAPTER 5

The Dynamics of Trustee Responsibility

In monitoring, evaluating, and ensuring accountability, the board needs to understand the culture of academic professionals and be well informed about the institution's academic programs. The knowledge required is not that of experts but includes an understanding of the basic logic of programs as capacities of the institution. How does the program relate to mission? What are its strategic goals? How is it evaluated?

The board needs to grasp the educational dynamic of programs and how they interact to create various degree options for students. Familiarity with academic language is important so that the board can evaluate the effectiveness of existing or new programs in fulfilling the institution's strategic goals. By attending to wider educational trends in teaching, learning, and the curriculum, trustees will be able to situate the distinctive program choices of their own institutions. An institution's academic identity is found precisely in how its constellation of programs sets it apart from others.

Trustee knowledge is not passive but is put to use in a continual *monitoring* of academic programs and policies, all of which are works in progress. Programs are in constant motion as students and faculty members enter and depart, as new courses are added and others dropped, and as entire new pedagogical approaches and programs are proposed. The governing board actively monitors this changing scene by persistently posing strategic and fundamental questions, an array of which appear in previous chapters. In practice, the questions will take on the coloring of the specific circumstances of each institution, even as they boil down to such issues as consistency with mission, integration with other programs, efficiency in the use of resources, assessment of results, alignment with strategic goals, and distinctiveness and quality of programs.

Many times, trustees and others within and outside the academy disparage trustee monitoring of the academic program. It is portrayed as a passive formality or, worse, as a wasted effort in which trustees are expected to rubber stamp the administration's and faculty's proposals.

Effective monitoring as an active process of inquiry offers more promising potential. When those in the chain of decision making realize that the institution's highest authority will pose fundamental and penetrating questions, the entire process is changed. Department leaders, deans, and provosts will create more rigorous and thoughtful proposals to fit the context of the anticipated questions they know will be coming. Both by the reality and the symbolism of the authority they hold, trustees who engage in this active monitoring process set in motion a continuing process of responsiveness and of responsibility. Thus, it becomes one of the ways the board participates in the collaborative leadership of the institution.

As the board monitors the academic program it also *evaluates* the institution's performance. To do so effectively, it operates on two levels. First, the board ensures that the faculty and administration have developed a self-conscious series of methods to gather and analyze information about the academic program. And second, because the requirements of accreditation or of state agencies mean that every institution will have addressed the assessment issue in some form, trustees should be aware of the broad outlines of the processes the institution uses and confident that self-evaluation has become internalized as a continuing aspect of the institution's life.

Although the board is not expected to create or operate the processes of evaluation, it sees the results. It regularly should receive summaries of annual assessment reports, significant surveys and studies, program reviews, and analyses of progress in reaching strategic goals. As the administration gathers and prepares information for the board, it typically will offer its own interpretation of the results and of perceived strengths and weaknesses. Although the board should give substantial weight to these analyses, it also should bring its own independent judgment to bear. The board not only should receive evaluations from others, but it also should critically review, integrate, and interpret the meaning of the data from its own vantage point. By seeing the institution whole and exercising final responsibility for it, board members can discern issues not visible to those enmeshed in the process.

Because the board evaluates performance, it is able to *ensure accountability* for fulfilling the institution's purposes and achieving its strategic goals. In healthy organizations, assessment leads naturally to actions designed to improve performance. Good data beg to be used to make the place better. The board needs to make certain that the tie is tightly drawn between knowing and doing, between gathering information and using it to improve quality.

Finally, the board has to oversee and evaluate the process of implementing the strategies to reach established goals. Effective operational and strategic planning gives the board a rich agenda for review. Has the institution taken the proposed actions? Are they working? Are goals being met? Are new or altered goals needed? If not, what new designs are being considered to solve the problem?

If significant commitments are not being met, then the board has cause to involve itself with the administration and faculty to mobilize initiatives and require new actions. Precisely how to do so requires careful reflection to ensure consistency with institutional culture and practices. That topic will be considered later in this chapter through two case studies, as well as in a discussion of the work of the academic affairs committee in a subsequent chapter.

The Decision-Making Process

In addition to monitoring, evaluating, and ensuring accountability for academic programs, boards have to make decisions affecting them. At most institutions, board action is the final step in the creation or discontinuation of academic programs. Boards of large institutions make decisions about programs at virtually every meeting, while those of small colleges may make such decisions only a handful of times in a decade.

Boards rarely initiate program decisions. Rather, they receive proposals that have been through an elaborate process of review, deliberation, and recommendation by departments, schools, deans, chief academic officers, and the president. As they raise and answer the key questions related to new programs, faculty and administrators should be expected to address issues of financing, staffing, student demand, program quality, and strategic fit. If the proposed program represents an entirely new type of degree for the institution—the addition of a bachelor's of science program, for example—then it will be considered a "substantive change," and accreditation review will be part of the process.

Like the board's responsibility to monitor and evaluate existing programs, its decision-making role first involves trustees becoming confident that the process that has brought the proposal to the board is sound and thorough. Prior knowledge by faculty and administration of the board's standards, expectations, and active assessment of proposals will build a higher level of rigor and coherence into whatever program is brought forward.

Should the board's review of the proposal raise substantive questions on financial, strategic, or even on content grounds, the board has a variety of options. Typically, a board would ask the administration and faculty to answer questions addressing certain serious issues before reconsidering the proposal. As the case studies will explore, the specific tactics for handling the deferral, revision, or rejection of a program will vary by institution. The board will not want to embarrass those who have recommended the proposal to the board (typically the president or provost). In urging further consideration of a proposal, the board will be at pains to differentiate the issues so that its concerns or questions do not appear to be a repudiation of substantive academic judgment made at prior levels. If this occurs, the board will face a difficult burden of proof in substituting its judgment for that of academic experts. In the rare instances where a board might contemplate such an action, the board itself should seek professional opinions as a basis for its decision to reject a program.

When the board is asked to make a final decision to discontinue an existing program, its review may require special procedures. If the program to be eliminated involves the termination of faculty or staff appointments, particularly tenured positions, the decision becomes far more complex. Normally, institutions will have established procedures, usually involving direct board involvement, to ensure that all sides of the issue have been explored, all parties heard, and all procedures scrupulously followed. Chapter 6 examines these questions in greater detail and suggests issues about which board members should be especially mindful.

Some critics of the prevailing patterns of academic decision making argue that boards should exercise their final authority over the curriculum much more fully and freely than normally is the case. Boards should be able to shape curricular content by initiating change and defining program requirements, they argue. Indeed, from time to time, boards do act directly to specify curricular requirements. Board intervention might be anticipated in institutions under the control of a religious denomination, for example. More controversially, however, the motive of some boards seems to be a desire to place greater curricular emphasis on Western civilization in an effort to balance its perceived neglect within contemporary higher education.[1]

Because the board possesses the authority to do so, should it not impose curricular requirements when it conscientiously believes it has justifiable cause to act? As is often the case, pursuing the question in abstract terms of legal authority may lead in the wrong direction. Boards can do countless things legally that are stunningly unwise or prohibited on other grounds. They legally can hire presidents with no involvement whatsoever of any other constituency, but no board would do so if it wants the new president to enjoy support. Boards legally can employ faculty by acting alone, but not if they wish to abide by standards for accreditation. Individual board members legally can give money to impoverished student athletes, but not if they want their institution to be a member of the National Collegiate Athletic Association.

What these illustrations suggest is that the board exercises its academic responsibilities in a world of multiple expectations and authorities, prevailing understandings of good practice, and attendant regulatory and legal limitations. To contravene authoritative understandings of sound professional practice is to court recrimination and to invite redress.

On campus, the implications of imposing curricular decisions cut in different directions. In a modern college or university, the board's legal authority in everything from accounting standards to student disciplinary proceedings is filtered through multiple layers of defined practice and procedure. State and federal law create a thick net of requirements and duties. Board bylaws and faculty handbooks define policies and procedures through which the board has limited itself, including the way it exercises its own legal authority. The board has the authority to change the procedures, but until it does

DATA POINT

34% of respondents said the board regularly plays a decision-making role in the general education curriculum, either by giving final approval to proposals or by providing advice and comment. **41%** said curricular matters are presented to the board for information only. **23%** said such matters do not come to the board at all. **87%** said individual course approval is not a board issue.

so it is bound by them. In effect, the board's authority to act independently in the academic and other spheres may be less than some trustees expect.

Regardless of the board's actual legal authority, there is a steep price to pay for disrupting the normal expectations of the academic decision-making process. In the eyes of the faculty, whose view is supported by a large body of expert opinion and the weight of respected traditions, the curriculum is its realm of primary responsibility. If the board is perceived as invading this sphere, the problem becomes an ethical one. In interceding, the board communicates disrespect for the faculty's professional identity and integrity and violates the established norms of collaborative academic decision making. The result will be faculty distrust and resentment that will undercut cooperation long into the future.

Finally, in a modern university that operates with the full protections of academic freedom, a board that seeks to impose a curricular mandate might ask itself what it really hopes to achieve. Whatever program or requirement the board may impose, it is the faculty, the people "on the ground" who will deliver the lectures, lead the discussions, choose the readings, develop the assignments, grade the papers, and assess the students. The professor has to be free to challenge students and their ideas and to question critically every text. Much of what students learn will be a function of what the professor takes to be important. However significant the curriculum, more important are the faculty members who teach it. They are not subject to intellectual mandates.

So, the question about the board's possible intervention in the curriculum seems to answer itself. Under most scenarios, it is a bad idea. It may even be a dangerous idea if ideological or political influences press a board to interfere in the curriculum. The board's first responsibility is always to the well-being of the institution, and efforts from special interests to control the board's conduct, especially if motivated by ideology, can undermine academic integrity. If boards or other stakeholders are convinced that the curriculum is in ideological disarray, they have a variety of ways to respond. The answer, however, is not to install its own curriculum.

The primary issue is not the board's authority but the use it makes of that authority. When it uses its authority to ask powerful questions, to require effective methods of evaluation, and to expect the results of assessment to translate into continuing efforts at improving performance, the board can have a decisive and enduring impact on educational quality. When it holds the administration and faculty responsible for reaching strategic goals, it puts its authority to work as a crucial part of a process of collaborative decision making and institutional leadership. In that case, the board is making a critical difference as it exercises its academic responsibilities.

Abstract terms such as "authority" and "responsibility" become easier to understand if considered in light of two case studies. Both are hypothetical, but both combine elements of actual cases.

Case 1: Crisis in General Education in a Liberal Arts College

A private undergraduate liberal arts college of 1,800 students has established a strategic goal of developing a new general education program. The college offers several successful professional programs in addition to 24 majors in the arts and sciences and has competitive but not selective admissions standards. The current "breadth" requirement consists mainly of introductory survey courses combining lectures with discussion sessions. Studies have shown that students are critical of the program because it repeats work done in high school. They complain that the courses are not interesting, that the discussions do not relate to the lectures, that choices to meet requirements are too limited, and that most of the tests and assignments require them simply to give back information.

Attrition after the freshman and sophomore years is notably higher than predicted by student test scores and high school grades, with exit interviews of departing students showing discontent with the courses in the first two years as the third most important reason students transfer. The data show that a high proportion of the most talented students transfer, often because they are disappointed with their experience.

The institution's finances are stable, but it is highly tuition dependent, and past financial problems have occurred because of enrollment declines. A reduction in attrition rates is a central aspect of the strategic plan's financial model to attain long-term financial equilibrium through modest enrollment growth.

After two years of labor, the college's curriculum committee has not produced a program the faculty supports. Conflicts within the committee between personalities and over educational philosophy, including skirmishes in the "culture wars," have stalled the work. The administration has cooperated with the committee but has not pressed for any given program, fearing that it then would become the "administration's proposal." One compromise plan is brought before the faculty for a straw vote, but responses in campus discussions and on the floor of the faculty senate show no widespread support. Faculty members complain that the proposed new requirements cannot be staffed with existing faculty and resources, and the administration cannot promise additional funds. Some department chairs privately complain that they see the proposal as a threat to future enrollments, and hence to staffing levels.

In a review of the goals of the strategic plan, the board's academic affairs committee learns of the problems with the general education proposal, and committee members review the issue at length with the president, the chief academic officer, and faculty leaders. Everyone knows the vital importance of the issue and is frustrated with the situation. They are open to new approaches, though they also are sensitive to the academic self-governance traditions of the faculty and its curriculum committee. The board always has believed that the curriculum should be left to the faculty.

After a long, private conversation with the president, and with his diffident concurrence, the committee chair proposes that it is time to develop a specific charge from the committee for the whole board to consider. Preceded by a pointed and probing discussion of the unusual step they are about to take, the board adopts a resolution addressed to the president but intended for the academic administration and the faculty as well. To foster this wider communication, the board circulates its resolution to the entire faculty.

The board frames its resolution in terms of the strategic goal previously endorsed by all parties to develop a new general education program and summarizes its deliberations in assessing the achievement of the goal. The information related to student attrition is placed in the context of the board's commitment to academic quality and to the institution's financial future—issues the board sees as strategically inseparable. The board explains that if the institution's long-term academic, strategic, and financial objectives are to be met, then enrollment levels must be enlarged, and attrition must be reduced. Respectful of the prior efforts by the faculty and the administration, the board calls for a new effort to develop an approach to general education that responds to problems that have been discovered in various assessments. The board establishes a broad expectation for a forward-looking program using the best pedagogical practices, a balance of studies attending to classic texts from both the Western tradition and other cultures, and a clear and thoughtful rationale for course requirements. It charges the president, academic administrators, and faculty leaders to accomplish the task through existing or special committees, as they judge best.

The board sets a deadline of one academic year for a new program to be developed and approved, with new courses phased in over time, according to a schedule to be devised by the administration and faculty. The board asks for progress reports to be submitted prior to each board meeting and for the chair and other members of the committee developing the program to meet with the president and the board's academic affairs committee when the board convenes. The board requests the president to make general education a strategic funding priority.

The board's resolution electrifies the campus since it runs counter to their tradition of distancing themselves from curricular questions. Many of the faculty in professional fields approve of the board's action, because they have been critical of what they see as the endless bickering of their colleagues in the liberal arts. Most of the senior faculty in arts and sciences are deeply disturbed, and many are angered over what they believe is a violation of the traditions of academic decision making. Whatever the intent, the board has communicated loss of confidence in the faculty and administration and disrespect for the faculty role in governance. There is talk of faculty "boycotting" the whole process of general education reform. A number of faculty committee chairs request a meeting with the president, the board chair, and the chair of the academic affairs committee, which is granted.

The faculty leaders criticize the board's action, repeating the concerns that have been circulating on campus. They ask that the resolution be rescinded or amended to remove references, even in broad terms, to desired forms of pedagogy or expected course content. They further indicate that deadlines and interim reports do not fit the way a faculty develops a curriculum. They are offensive tactics of the corporate world that have no place in academe.

The air is tight with tension when the board chair speaks bluntly and with some emotion to open the meeting. He says that it appears that the faculty wants to be accountable to no one for anything, not even to themselves for commitments they have made. The board cannot build a little white picket fence around the campus to keep the faculty safe and secure from the real world. He emphasizes that keeping good students and funding the college are the central goals. The board has a final responsibility for the good of the whole college that it cannot delegate to anyone else.

Seeing several faces flush with anger, the chair of the academic affairs committee tries to reposition the discussion. She indicates that her committee was sensitive to all of the faculty's concerns and discussed them with the faculty on the committee, as well as with the president and the chief academic officer. The resolution that was adopted was criteria-referenced to the college's traditions of governance under these serious circumstances. She goes on to illustrate her claim. The reform of general education is on the college's strategic agenda by prior action of all the college's decision-making bodies, including the whole faculty. She emphasizes that before acting, the committee considered an array of information, including the curriculum committee's various proposals. She argues that the committee intended to craft a proposal that drew a wide circle around the issues without intending to prescribe or dictate curricular content to the faculty. All the references in the resolution to pedagogies and content questions came from the curriculum committee's prior proposals and background papers.

By establishing broad expectations, she says, the board's committee is not legislating a program but simply trying to move the process forward. The faculty is still free to exercise its best judgment, even to interpret differently the resolution's "broad expectations," as long as it meets its responsibility to create an effective general education program. The chair ends her remarks by asking the faculty whether some of them might not be responding more to appearance than reality. She notes that if the faculty were carefully to define and differentiate roles and responsibilities in academic decision making, as might be done by scholars analyzing this situation, they would conclude that the board's action is an example of appropriate self-limitation in the use of its authority.

A more cooperative tone begins to shape the conversation, as the president tries to sum up his feelings. He notes that he before anyone else should resent the board's resolution, and he did so initially. He says that he keeps racking his brain wondering what he could have done to avoid this impasse. He wonders aloud whether this would have happened if he had more political skills. Finally, though, he has concluded that though he carries formal responsibility for the academic program, he does not have the authority to fulfill that responsibility. Academic authority rests with the faculty. He also believes that had he struck the alarm bell without the board's involvement, his actions would have been stereotyped as administrative interference or worse.

Although he did not like the board's charging him to act under a deadline—nor did he appreciate the board communicating with everyone as it did—he has come to believe it represents both a wise and legitimate action by the board. He will not now be accused of putting words in the mouth of the board, as has happened in the past. Most important, he has learned that you cannot define a decision-making role for the board in academic affairs and then be unhappy if its members exercise it. We tell the academic affairs committee and the board to evaluate the academic program, the president says, and to make us answerable for the goals that we have set in the educational program. That is what the board did.

The case continues. After many meetings with the chief academic officer, representatives of the faculty governing council, and the chair of the curriculum committee, it is proposed to the president that a new committee be created to develop a proposal. The new committee examines a series of model programs and invites several national leaders on general education to consult with the committee. The new proposal fits the framework established by the board, though the committee's work evolves according to its own insights and rhythms. At the final meeting of the academic year, the new program is adopted by a majority of the faculty, with some abstaining in protest over the process. The academic affairs committee discusses and endorses the new program and reports to the full board on its contents. There is a discussion as to whether the full board needs to act officially, given that the degree program is not a new one. The decision is made to adopt a resolution of approval because it changes degree requirements for all students. The board unanimously adopts the resolution.

This case illustrates the way a board actively carries out its role in monitoring, evaluating, ensuring accountability of, and making decisions about academic programs. Readers are encouraged to consider their own responses to this situation. Does this case represent effective or ineffective work by trustees? Do they go too far or not far enough?

What specific factors about the institution are most relevant in the interpretation of the case? Do the board's actions meet the criterion of legitimacy? Were the senior faculty's initial criticisms valid or misplaced? How would you have responded to the board as president of the institution? As chair of the academic affairs committee, how would you have handled the situation?

Case 2: Academic Exigency

To illustrate another set of possibilities for board involvement, let us change the facts of the prior case to create extreme circumstances. Everything unfolds the same way, except that the faculty turns down the committee's proposal, and rejects it a second time when asked to reconsider it by the president and the board. It happens that the board's intervention and discord over the place of the Western tradition in a proposed humanities sequence were much more ideological and bitter than anticipated. Open hostility destroys the process.

At the board meeting where these developments are reviewed, the chair of the academic affairs committee advances a bold argument. She claims that the mission and strategic prospects of the institution are intimately tied to the effectiveness of the general education program. The board has demonstrated its convictions by its actions. The faculty's failure cannot be allowed to stand, lest the board forsake its fiduciary responsibilities. She goes on to argue that the failure is not the responsibility of the administration, because it does not have the authority that it would possess in a tightly coupled, hierarchical decision-making system. Rather, it is time to develop a new concept, a kind of "academic exigency" parallel to "financial exigency," but with nothing to do with tenure. Academic exigency means to her that after following stringent procedures to safeguard the normal processes of academic decision making, the board can take an academic program into "receivership." The chair argues that the burden of proof to do so should be high and demonstrably related to central issues of mission and institutional viability. Once valid information has been studied, the issues defined, external mediation sought and completed, all parties heard, and final efforts to resolve the problems attempted, the board can address academic program issues directly through its own powers and authority. It may declare exigency and then, as in this case, create a general education program through the authority it would delegate to the faculty and administration, outside experts, and members of its own board.

This extreme situation is not implausible, especially given recent developments on many campuses. In this case, though, the board has acted only after satisfying a rigorous set of procedures. How would the reader respond to a proposal to develop procedures for the equivalent of "academic bankruptcy?" If the board has the standing authority to take the action, to create a program anyway, why are new self-limiting procedures needed? Or to take a contrary view, does not the board's effective, if formal, authority stop at the classroom door? Do academic institutions have to live with whatever the academic professionals finally decide or refuse to decide, since their expertise and autonomy will control what and how anything is actually taught? What are the implications of the board's action? What should a president do in these circumstances?

Although this may be an unlikely scenario, it sharpens issues that recently have arisen

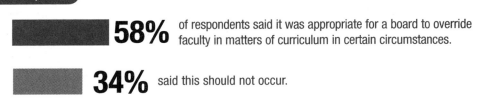

DATA POINT

58% of respondents said it was appropriate for a board to override faculty in matters of curriculum in certain circumstances.

34% said this should not occur.

in higher education. Given the tumult of life and the play of forces around ideological issues and partisan politics, it is wise to ponder and test ideas of trustee authority under various scenarios.

These two cases illustrate the variety of evaluations, judgments, and decisions in the work of the board. Although more complicated than normal decisions, they highlight the underlying processes and issues that may figure in board deliberations. The board's responsibilities to monitor, evaluate, and hold the administration and faculty accountable for results in the academic realm are consequential. These responsibilities represent a significant, often underappreciated opportunity for the board to contribute decisively, yet appropriately, to academic decision making.

[1] Schmidt, Peter. "SUNY Faculty Groups Lack Faith in Board," *Chronicle of Higher Education*, Vol. 46, no. 13 (May 14, 1999), page A40.

Magner, Denise K. "Battle Over Academic Control Pits Faculty Against Governing Board at George Mason U." *Chronicle of Higher Education* (June 18, 1999), page A14.

Magner, Denise K. "Faculty Accuses George Mason U. Board of Improper Meddling With Curriculum," *Chronicle of Higher Education* (June 2, 2000), page A20.

Shechner, Mark. "Ozymandias on the Erie: What Is It Like to Teach in a State Where Politicians No Longer Care About Public Higher Education?" *Academe*, Vol. 86, no. 6 (November/December 2000), pages 24-33.

CHAPTER 6

Faculty Responsibilities and Tenure and Appointment Policies

To deepen their understanding of the culture of academic professionals, trustees should consider how the faculty form their values as they prepare to enter the profession and then how those values play out on the job. Such an analysis will leave trustees in a better position to analyze tenure and alternatives to it. This chapter is intended to help.

Although the tracks vary in some fields, the standard pathway to a career as a professor is the completion of a doctoral degree, usually a Ph.D. Requiring full-time study beyond the baccalaureate level of at least four to six years, but often much longer, the experience of earning a Ph.D. is intensely demanding both intellectually and personally. As never before in their earlier studies, graduate students must learn the strict requirements of specialized research. The joy of learning encounters the protocols of professionalized disciplines.

Simultaneous with intellectual training, graduate students undergo a process of socialization. They master the ins and outs of their chosen disciplines and come to identify themselves as historians, sociologists, or physicists. They learn a new language that distinguishes their profession from others, creating bonds with those who understand the same technical terms. Living for periods of time as modern ascetics, graduate students undertake demanding and often solitary research projects that culminate in the Ph.D. thesis, an elaborate work of original research. In the process, they are socialized to a specific set of values. They learn that the formulation, articulation, and defense of one's own ideas and findings are the *sine qua non* of the academic profession. Critical thought becomes a cardinal virtue, including the ability to direct penetrating criticism against opposing interpretations. Academic professionals are socialized to independent judgment, intellectual freedom, professional autonomy, identification with the colleagues in one's field, and to a commitment to expand knowledge through research. The orientation to research is intrinsic to the design of the doctorate. Those who perform it well become recognized in the profession.

The next stage in the life of the young academic professional is often disorienting because the demands of the first appointment to a faculty position require a rapid shift in professional gears from research to teaching. The nearly exclusive focus on research in graduate study, with apprentice teaching typically incidental to the experience, creates values and expectations that clash with the reality of the new position. With a few happy exceptions, undergraduates are bored or mystified by the young scholar's specialized research and unappreciative of the new teacher's exalted expectations. Although many efforts continue to include preparation for teaching in graduate education, the challenge of changing the intense research culture of doctoral study has yet to be met.

What then is the transition that the young professor must make to be an effective campus citizen? Observing the work of more seasoned colleagues, the newcomer takes note of their capacity to handle several competing expectations and responsibilities simultaneously. The continuation of a research agenda usually is a given; this is an essential goal of the individual and an expectation, in varying degrees, of the institution. Yet now the new instructor's research responsibilities must be combined with effective teaching, an extraordinarily time-consuming commitment. This involves creating a whole repertoire of courses, perhaps five or six new offerings in the first year or two of teaching. Continuing contact with students and the design and grading of assignments consume huge blocks of time that conflict with the demands of research.

The new teacher's role also will require various forms of institutional service beyond teaching and research. It may mean participation as an academic adviser, an important responsibility for which he or she has received no preparation. The business of the department is an inescapable duty, and if curricular changes are in order, then planning and consultation with colleagues are constant. The wider work of campus governance also may beckon, as college or university committees press their claims. Sometimes relieved from some of these duties until after the tenure decision, the young scholar still learns the multiple roles that define faculty work. The pressure of being pulled in three or four directions at once can be energizing but disorienting.

Amid these conflicting demands, the newcomer also learns that the faculty reward system, depending on the institution, seems to favor published research, no matter what the institution's formal documents proclaim. Many faculty members believe deeply that only research truly counts in tenure, promotion, and salary decisions.

Nonetheless, even with these heavy and competing demands, faculty report more fulfillment than frustration with their work, embrace their profession, and work hard at it—an average of 50-55 hours a week, as studies consistently show.[1]

Trustees should be aware that efforts are underway on some campuses to think more creatively about how faculty work should be defined in the future. Teaching, research, and service are each becoming more complex and variable. The common unit of work load measurement, however, has largely been invariant, with a certain number of course-credit or contact hours defining a faculty member's responsibilities. Now, teaching is changing, as the supervision of student research, collaborative projects, or internships accounts for a growing share of a faculty member's time. Increasingly, teaching involves designing

courses to exploit technology or creating and evaluating complex assignments to better involve
students in learning. Few institutions, however,
have developed policies that reflect what these new
roles mean for the definition of faculty responsibility.[2] Similarly, research increasingly is a highly
variable activity, both in the different phases of a
person's career and among faculty members.

Should these different patterns be recognized as
part of different cycles in an individual's career,
with relatively low teaching demands for one period alternating with high teaching loads
at another? How do appointment and work-load patterns play to the diverse strengths
that individuals bring to their work in teaching, scholarship and institutional service?
These and related questions define emerging issues that faculty and administrators should
explore with the encouragement of the governing board.

DATA POINT

30% of respondents said
their institutions discussed policies
on faculty work load in the past
five years. **37%** of public
institutions and **18%** of privates
discussed these policies.

Tenure, Academic Freedom, and Security

Trustees who comprehend the ways faculty members prepare for and conceive of their
responsibilities will have a clearer view as to why tenure is one of the defining tenets of
the academic profession. The classical statement on tenure is found in the American
Association of University Professors' (AAUP) 1940 "Statement of Principles." Tenure is "a
means to certain ends; specifically: (1) freedom of teaching and research and of extramural
activities, and (2) a sufficient degree of economic security to make the profession attractive to men and women of ability. Freedom and economic security, hence, tenure, are
indispensable to the success of an institution in fulfilling its obligations to its students and
to society."[3]

The statement asserts that freedom to inquire and communicate defines the academic
profession. Tenure guarantees freedom as a condition necessary to teaching and research
in a free society. The economic security of tenure attracts people to a profession that
requires commitment to a long period of training and subsequent specialized practice.
For some, the prospect of tenure justifies the lengthy preparation and intense specialization that means foregoing other livelihoods. As tenure has developed in this country and
others, it is understood in terms of academic freedom and employment security. Tenure
enables the practice of the academic profession that in turn is essential to the well-being
of a democratic and free society. Those who support tenure see it as necessary for the
protection of values that enable the practice of the profession as we have known it in the
modern era.[4]

The idea of tenure always stirs passions, which rise and fall with the economic and
social realities of the wider world. In the late 1960s, media images of scruffy, activist
professors inciting civil disobedience or campus turmoil filled the public mind and
created hostility toward a group perceived as untouchable. Twenty years later, as American

business recaptured its economic self-confidence even while eliminating thousands of positions, the job guarantees of tenure seemed to many to be the private possession of an elite class.

Many trustees will confess privately and sometimes publicly that they are troubled and perplexed by the tenure system. They see institutions struggling to introduce new programs, reduce expenses, and improve quality while being prevented from eliminating positions held by highly compensated tenured faculty. The services of some of those individuals no longer may be needed, and in some cases, their work may have become mediocre or worse. These friendly critics know and appreciate the arguments about the importance of academic freedom and job security, yet they suggest that legal protections, contractual guarantees, and accreditation requirements make it extremely unlikely that a faculty member will be terminated for exercising academic freedom. They assert that colleges, like every other organization in society, must deal more effectively with bitter economic realities in order to produce greater long-term quality and effectiveness.

How are trustees to think about tenure? As with most questions of this kind, there is no way to settle the question abstractly because arguments for or against tenure depend upon unprovable assumptions. Although we lack the evidence to know what would happen under various social and economic circumstances without the guarantees of tenure, it is possible to speculate about likely consequences. Amid the pervasive influence of single-issue politics and polemics in our political and social lives, we can wonder what might happen in classrooms and to published research without the strong protections of tenure. Heavily financed and mobilized activism at both ends of the political spectrum could find new targets of opportunity on campuses that eschewed tenure. Professors, vulnerable at the time of contract renewal, could find themselves the objects of intense and orchestrated hostility. Pretextual terminations might become common.

Also, the easy confidence many maintain that the courts will protect academic freedom may be foolhardy. First, there are no constitutional protections for freedom of speech or due process in private institutions. It is conceivable that in complex cases courts would be unable to sort out academic freedom from other grounds for termination, such as budgetary constraint, that could serve as the pretext for a decision detrimental to free expression. Whatever else, there would be wide variations in court decisions in various jurisdictions, creating a legal patchwork of uncertainty and anxiety.

An ironic but persuasive argument in favor of tenure is that although it may have a role in protecting academic freedom from external sources, its most vital contribution is protecting academics from one another. Though the irony has to be kept in mind, departments and programs frequently divide around various fault lines of personal rivalries, clashing interpretations of the nature of the discipline, and disagreements over the quality of one another's work. On at least a few campuses, the battles in the "culture wars" probably would yield mortal casualties absent the protections of tenure. Were conflicts of this kind to come into play in decisions about the renewal of long-term contracts (as an alternative to tenure), the results could lead to some punitive decisions and perpetual warfare.

For some trustees, another persuasive argument for tenure is that such a decision is so significant that it forces institutions to make demanding choices. Tenure is consistent with whatever standards institutions choose, and the logic of the decision leads to high expectations. Appointment to tenure means literally that an institution is committing its resources for a person's professional lifetime. When doing so, it should be confident that the candidate for a permanent appointment has shown a superior level of achievement and potential that others available to fill the position could not easily exceed.

Tenure and the Elimination of Mandatory Retirement

It's easy to criticize tenure during difficult financial times when institutions are required to cut positions and drop programs. Without question, tenure seriously complicates an institution's ability to handle fiscal stress. In this regard, one reason tenure recently has come under greater scrutiny is the elimination of mandatory retirement for tenured faculty. The problem is not the prohibition of a specific retirement age but that the guarantees of tenure can continue indefinitely. In the original legislation eliminating mandatory retirement, the Age Discrimination in Employment Act, higher education was exempted from the application of the law during a period of declining enrollment. It was judged that during this time there would be few new openings for faculty members starting their careers. Yet when the exemption ended in 1994, the anticipated growth in faculty hiring did not materialize in most fields, and opportunities for new professors have continued to be limited. Early retirement plans have addressed some of the problems related to the elimination of a fixed retirement age, and a long-anticipated wave of faculty retirements soon will create a good deal more flexibility and opportunity for new faculty appointments. The critique of tenure may diminish as institutions are able to reshape their faculty profiles.

There is no question that when the tenure system lacks a required point of exit, it complicates the already vexing problem of creating openings for new faculty. It limits the opportunity to hire faculty members from underrepresented groups or to appoint individuals trained in newer methods or fields. From a financial perspective, the absence of fixed retirement ages means the higher costs of salaries for senior faculty members are likely to continue for longer periods.

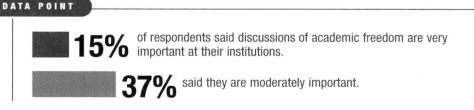

DATA POINT

15% of respondents said discussions of academic freedom are very important at their institutions.

37% said they are moderately important.

Alternatives Within Tenure Policies

The term "tenure" itself tends to cloud the mind, so thick are its fixed associations. Yet tenure is a contract between an institution and an individual. Its terms and conditions, absent any requirements of state law, are created by the institution itself. In other words, there are no legal or regulatory standards for tenure, except the requirements to which institutions bind themselves as they define tenure and establish related procedures. An institution is free to develop an appointment system that does not include tenure, or it can create tenure provisions that fit its circumstances. In fact, few institutions seem to be aware of the substantial flexibility and alternative policy options that exist within tenure. At its base, tenure is simply a continuous appointment that can be terminated for adequate cause.

There are various reasons for the development of a common mindset about tenure and related procedures. One of these is that for a long time, most institutions relied heavily on the model policies of the AAUP. Institutions would incorporate language and even detailed policies from AAUP documents, so tenure definitions and procedures had a common shape across the country.

AAUP's policies and procedures are thoughtful, carefully crafted, and worth examining. Yet trustees, administrators, and faculty members should know that incorporating detailed policies and procedures from an external source into an institution's tenure documents can create unintended consequences. It may create the expectation that the outside authority has been chosen to function as the normative standard for the institution's policies. If institutions include texts and policies from another source in their own materials, they should carefully define and limit the context in which such policies apply.

Can tenure be modified or even abandoned? Challenging an existing tenure system wholesale is possible, but it is likely to be a highly emotional and divisive step that takes inordinate time. Because tenure is a contract, it cannot be revoked unilaterally, so it will continue in force until those who hold tenure choose to resign or to retire.

Even though most institutions may choose not to challenge tenure itself, they periodically should revisit their tenure provisions. The goal would be to clarify procedures and update definitions of such issues as professional incompetence, moral turpitude, financial exigency, and program discontinuance. These are the traditional factors that may lead to the termination of tenured appointments for adequate cause. These categories often have been in documents for many years and may have become opaque, losing their meaning or their actionable significance. The notion that "you cannot touch" anyone who has tenure is inaccurate, and revisions and

> **DATA POINT**
>
> **45%** of respondents said their institutions discussed new tenure and promotion policies in the past five years. **40%** said the policies would be established by the administration after consultation with the board. **14%** said the board alone would establish the policies.

clarifications of policies can make that clear. Boards should encourage periodic policy reviews, especially relating to "adequate cause."

If, for instance, a university has become a true international leader in research, it might need to clarify its definitions of professional incompetence. Because it has long used demanding standards for research and publication in awarding tenure, it may need to adjust the meaning of adequate cause to account for its higher expectations concerning faculty research achievements. The understanding of incompetence or professional unfitness necessarily varies widely among different institutions with drastically diverse missions and expectations of faculty.

Clarification also is needed on issues of ethical misconduct, program discontinuance, and financial exigency. Boards should ask that the meaning of these terms be spelled out because circumstances differ so much among institutions. If, for example, "exigency" means "imminent bankruptcy," financial remedies might be applied only too late because the burden of proof is so high. On the other hand, if the institution has defined exigency as financial conditions that threaten failure in a designated time period, it is possible to have bona fide tests and measures that justify tenure reductions after the application of fair and proper procedures. The institution is free to adopt any coherent and reasonable standard. In a situation such as this, the old adage that "an ounce of prevention is worth a pound of cure" proves eminently true. Once a financial crisis begins, it is too late to change a policy to deal with it.

The issue of program discontinuance, the most common occasion for adequate-cause terminations, also requires careful definition. Are programs equivalent to departments, or are they courses of study in which a degree is offered, or are they defined subject areas that may or may not lead to a degree? For example, foreign languages sometimes each have their own departments, while at other times they may be grouped into a common department that offers degrees in several, but not all, languages. The question should be posed in advance hypothetically as to how the policy of program discontinuation would apply in these circumstances. For valid reasons relating to program quality or strategic priorities, is it possible to drop instruction in one language and with it tenured positions? Or does the institution need to drop the whole department to count as program discontinuation? Institutions should define these issues for themselves.

Because program discontinuance offers only a narrow base for adequate-cause actions, some institutions have introduced different language to make clear that the institution can have much more flexibility. In addition to discontinuance, program modification can be specified as adequate cause. In other cases, institutions tie potential action to drop tenured positions to the elimination of the work that a faculty member was hired to perform. Operating within the confines of tenure, institutional officials have much more flexibility to respond to strategic issues and changing academic circumstances than they may think.

The effort to clarify tenure provisions also will require a close look at the procedures used in terminations for adequate cause. Frequently, it is not the language defining tenure or termination that puts a brake on action but the elaborateness and Byzantine complexity of the termination procedures. Procedures for program discontinuation and financial exigency sometimes are similarly ornate. Here again, the institution is free to craft procedures that are fair to individuals while also protecting the long-term well-being of the institution as a whole.

Many campuses are reluctant to review tenure provisions because the issue can be so sensitive and create deep suspicion. One way to address these realities is for trustees to request a regular, periodic review of tenure documents. As legal issues and institutional circumstances continuously evolve, a regular review of fundamental policies is entirely appropriate. Another possibility is to relate a policy review to a strategic analysis of the institution's overall situation. If specific standards and procedures for tenure are to be examined as part of strategic planning (a common practice), it makes sense to review all tenure provisions. Each part of the system relates to the other. A review may or may not lead to proposals for change, but it is a necessary first step in this highly charged arena.

The board's role in considering tenure and related faculty personnel policies is a vital one in several ways. In addition to reviewing and acting on fundamentally important policies, board members themselves may become decision makers in disputed cases. For example, the board typically is the "court of last resort" in tenure removal for adequate cause. The board normally would make the final decision in specific cases, receiving recommendations from the president and/or a faculty committee. Because of its potential to become directly involved in such cases, the board has every reason to change, add, or create language in policies that define its involvement.

Tenure Quotas

As an era of strong enrollment growth in American higher education came to a close in the late 1970s, faculty expansion slowed, and mobility decreased. Almost overnight, the issue surfaced of faculties becoming "tenured in." To keep the system open, some institutions instituted "quota" systems to guarantee that no more than a set percentage of the faculty in a department, school, or college could hold tenure.

Although 13 percent of institutions continue to retain such quotas, experience has shown that tenure levels usually can be managed without the arbitrary controls and distortions such quotas introduce. If institutions have high standards for reappointment and tenure that are applied consistently throughout the provisional period of faculty appointments, then vacancies normally occur. After three or four years of the provisional period, faculty members and the institution generally will become aware if the match will be for

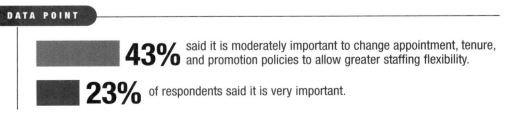

the long-term. At the other end of the system, there will be exits through resignation and retirement. Although such departures are not always predictable, especially given the elimination of mandatory retirement, the system is not closed. In sum, with just moderate attrition patterns and normal retirements, the system cannot exceed a maximum 75 percent rate of tenure.[5]

Temporary Appointments

Many institutions have chosen to guarantee some flexibility in tenure by creating one or more rotating or "non-tenure-track" positions in a department, depending on its size. The position may be renewable annually up to a stated maximum of three to six years. These non-tenure-track positions sometimes are essential to preserving flexibility in light of the rigidities of the tenure system, especially in a low-growth or no-growth environment. They bring in faculty with new ideas and allow institutions to plan carefully where they will invest their permanent resources. Temporary appointments are claiming an ever-larger share of the total faculty, raising many issues for the profession, institutions, and short-term faculty members. Data indicate that the percentage of non-tenure-track faculty increased from 21 percent to 29 percent from 1975 to 1993.[6]

Such rotating positions may or may not be in the best interest of institutions or the instructors. In some situations, faculty members with temporary appointments are buried under heavy teaching loads and find little opportunity to build their records of professional achievement. Often, faculty members become itinerants who move several times from one temporary position to another. In other cases, though, a temporary appointment can mark a useful opportunity for a person to develop teaching skills and publish research. Enlightened institutions will develop ways to recognize the contributions of temporary faculty and provide them with opportunities for professional development. In return, institutions are likely to have a more loyal and committed teacher who is not constantly preoccupied about finding time to search for the next job.

Part-Time Faculty

The increasing use of part-time faculty fits the picture of a low-growth faculty-employment system defined around the fixed point of tenure. Among the many reasons for part-time appointments are the desires to retain flexibility and lower instructional costs. Over the past 30 years, the percentage of faculty who teach part-time has doubled, rising to more than 40 percent. The highest proportions of part-time faculty, more than 60 percent, are in vocational fields in community colleges. These teachers often are employed full-time in other positions, whereas in many liberal arts fields part-time teachers tend to be those unable to find full-time employment. In four-year institutions, almost one-quarter of the professoriate is part-time, not counting graduate assistants.[7]

The use of part-timers raises questions of fairness. Some part-time teachers carry substantial loads and teach every year but do not qualify for benefits or participate in university governance. Many continuing part-timers are women, some of whom believe the system fails to provide equal opportunity. What's more, courses taught by teachers who constantly come and go may lack rigor, consistency, and quality. Finally, part-time teachers have little incentive to spend extra time with students or to devote long hours to designing and grading assignments.

In their review of tenure and related faculty employment policies, trustees will want to know the percentage, nature, and deployment of temporary and part-time positions. They will want to ensure that the institution's policies recognize the varying contributions of different forms of part-time service. If part-time appointments are increasing, represent a large proportion of the faculty, or consist heavily of single, rotating engagements, trustees will want to be shown how the institution guarantees the quality of instruction.

Post-Tenure Review

In response to criticisms of tenure, many institutions have developed post-tenure review policies, often as a result of requirements or recommendations by accrediting bodies or state systems. The goal of such reviews is to provide a systemic and comprehensive review every five to seven years for those who hold permanent appointments. Proponents of tenure review point out that other than annual salary reviews or reviews at the time of consideration for promotion to full professor, tenured professors never undergo systematic peer or administrative evaluation.[8]

The term "post-tenure review" strikes some as peculiar because it appears to suggest that a faculty member's tenure is being redecided. To be effective, post-tenure reviews obviously cannot be seen by faculty as a challenge to post-tenure itself. The goals of the process must be developed by faculty and administration working together, and the conclusions must be clearly worded. Tenure reviews typically are set in the context of professional development, self-assessment, and self-improvement. Information and opinions are gathered from a variety of sources, sometimes comparable in scope to what is collected for a tenure candidate. Unlike the tenure decision, in which the burden is on the individual to build a case for a permanent appointment, here the aim is to provide feedback on the person's performance. A committee of peers often systematically studies evaluations of the faculty member's teaching and scholarship. Out of the process may come any number of findings that are best conveyed in the framework of future professional development. Through the evaluation, a person considers how to build on past achievements, where to center future research activity, and how to improve effectiveness in teaching or ways to improve a curricular program.

How might an institution deal with serious deficiencies discovered through a tenure review? If the response is too direct and aggressive, the process may be seen as an attack on tenure. Yet institutions

DATA POINT

28% of survey respondents said it is very important to establish a plan for post-tenure review. **36%** said it is moderately important. **34%** said the issue had arisen in their institutions in the past five years.

cannot ignore serious performance problems. One strategy is to require that the individual develop a plan for improvement that focuses on specific goals to be achieved within a specified period. During that time, the institution would provide support and opportunities for the individual to remedy weaknesses. If serious issues persisted at the time of a subsequent annual salary review a year or two hence, the institution would have various options. An individual's assignments could be shifted to areas of greatest effectiveness, or the instructor could be strongly counseled to consider other career options. Or if the person has enough years of service, retirement or early retirement may be attractive choices. An incentive package, coupled perhaps with indications of a future of low or no raises, may lead many low-performing faculty to decide to resign or retire. Termination for cause also may be a possibility. The culture of the campus or department in responding to poor performance will determine the decision.

Performance reviews of faculty who hold tenure are logical components of a comprehensive approach to strategic evaluation. The downside becomes evident if a campus is filled with distrust, however. Depending on the effectiveness of existing patterns of annual salary reviews or other ways to monitor performance, trustees will want to explore with administrative and faculty leaders the possibility of a formal system of tenure review.

This discussion of post-tenure performance evaluations suggests that institutions can be much more creative and flexible when it comes to career counseling and financial planning for ineffective mid-career and late-career faculty. Were department chairs and deans to have more financial options to offer senior faculty—perhaps like those in the corporate world—there would be less concern over tenure and more ways to handle the problem of unproductive individuals. An irony in the critique of tenure by some business leaders is that corporations are far more generous to departing executives, even those at mid-levels, than colleges or universities ever could dream of being to faculty members.

Early Retirement

It used to be said, sometimes rather critically, that tenure constitutes a lifetime appointment. Today, the statement is literally true. Since the elimination of mandatory retirement, tenure, not just employment, continues without limit of time.

The tough issue for colleges and universities is not age or the fact of continuing employment without age limits. Rather, it is the removal of a fixed point of departure from a system of continuous, protected employment. What does this do to tenure? It adds challenges to an already complicated employment system. It drives up the cost of instruction by locking in the higher salaries associated with seniority, and it adds to the challenge of finding ways to make new appointments in departments that need them.

To address these complications, institutions increasingly have turned to using incentives for early retirement. Admittedly, the meaning of the phrase is elusive when there is no fixed retirement age. On the whole, faculty members may be retiring slightly later now than in the past, although the effects of the law prohibiting mandatory retirement are too recent to know why.[9] Also clouding the issues are the ways that early retirement incentives are now masking the motivation for retirement decisions.

In public institutions that participate in large-scale, state-funded, defined-benefit retirement plans, there are periodic early retirement offers linked to age and years of service. In general, defined-benefit plans tend to encourage retirement on economic grounds alone, because retirement benefits do not increase once a faculty member achieves a certain maximum years of service.

In 1998, the United States adopted into law a provision that allows participants in defined-contribution plans (like those sponsored by TIAA-CREF) to be given age-related retirement incentives, though persons of any age are required to be included in the plan the first time it is offered. Subsequently, individuals may be offered incentives that decline each year until a standard chronological age, at which point the incentives disappear. So, for example, faculty members might be given a lump-sum payment of 20 percent of salary for each year they retire prior to age 70 up to a stated maximum period. From a financial perspective, the plan is cost-neutral as long as the replacements for retiring faculty are hired at substantially lower rates, "reimbursing" the institution's capital outlay over a definable period of years. There are, of course, risks in the process. One may or may not gain value in the contributions of the replacement for the retiring member, and key contributors may be motivated to retire. In this context, early retirement has an "abstract" purpose. It becomes a way in which to open a door out of a closed system, allowing others to enter. Local patterns will determine how many doors need to be opened and what types of incentives are required.[10]

There are a number of other ways to encourage people to consider retirement in a system that no longer requires it. Various institutions offer programs of phased retirement or partial retirement, options that may become more significant in the future.

What many professors want most as they consider retirement is the opportunity to continue their work while they anticipate the freedom of a self-chosen schedule. Once a faculty member has achieved financial security, ties to the academic community and continuing relationships with colleagues are the most important considerations. Because of this, institutions may want to provide an equipped office, laboratory space, or carrel space in the library to help retirees share in campus life. There may be small courtesies and opportunities, from parking privileges to social occasions, that make the transition to retirement attractive for older faculty.

In many ways, the end of mandatory requirement suggests that the profession itself should develop a new ethic. If one has served a long and full career, has a strong financial base for retirement, and is in a field in which there are few vacancies for younger people, then retirement becomes a way to open up new opportunities for others. By affirming the future plans of retiring

DATA POINT

41% of respondents said their institutions had discussed early retirement programs for faculty during the past five years. **48%** of the publics and **39%** of the privates had such discussions.

faculty and their continuing ties to the institution, colleges and universities can advance this new ethic.

Alternatives to Tenure

Faculty personnel systems that offer alternatives to tenure are not new to higher education but have become more prevalent in recent decades. Small institutions and those with special missions are more likely to have abandoned tenure or never to have adopted it. Nonetheless, tenure decidedly remains the norm, with 81 percent of full-time faculty serving on campuses that offer tenure.

A typical alternative to tenure provides faculty members with long-term contracts that might range from three to ten years. Some institutions provide incentives—frequent sabbaticals, for example—to faculty who will forego tenure. According to higher education scholar Richard P. Chait, patterns of renewal and termination at the end of a contract period do not vary substantially from patterns of dismissals of faculty with tenure. A great majority of faculty members have their long-term contracts renewed.[11]

Because there are not enough examples of comparable institutions with and without tenure over long periods of time, one can only speculate about what might be the lasting consequences of the two different systems. Contract systems appear to have a high proportion of continuing reappointments, so one might surmise that neither tenure nor long-term contracts themselves constitute the most significant variable in producing continuing appointments. Rather, the values of academic professionals and the culture they create would explain both the existence of tenure itself as well as the likelihood of contract renewal. For peers not facing a tenure decision themselves, it is much easier psychologically, absent serious conflict, for most peers to recommend a colleague's contract be continued. Because the issue can be revisited in the future, there is a smaller burden in renewing a contract in a borderline case. Further, since one's own renewal may be just around the corner, there is a clear disincentive to create controversy among colleagues who will sit in judgment on one's own reappointment.

How peer review of contacts might play out during periods of internecine departmental conflict or retrenchment is unknown. Those whose contracts happen to be subject to renewal during an economic crisis may find themselves out of a job, creating a difficult anomaly for a contract system.

The attractiveness of contracts as alternatives to tenure obviously will depend on an institution's identity and strategy. Major research universities, and most selective colleges, probably would not find contracts effective in their efforts to attract and retain top scholars and scientists with international reputations. In the competition for talent, tenure or its equivalent is a given, and institutions without it are at a serious disadvantage. On the other hand, institutions that draw from surplus faculty employment markets or that are vulnerable financially may prefer contracts.

In considering tenure and alternatives within it or to it, governing board members will want to pose a variety of questions as they monitor and consider policies:

- When were the policies and procedures relating to termination of tenure for adequate cause last reviewed? What were the results?
- Have policies been adopted that limit the proportion of faculty who can hold tenure? What has been their effect?
- Does the institution use temporary or part-time appointments to provide flexibility within the tenure system? What numbers or percentages of temporary or part-time appointments are in place, what is their nature, and what do assessments of their effectiveness reveal?
- Has the institution developed a process of post-tenure review? If so, how does it work, and what are its results?
- Does the institution have an early retirement plan for faculty? If so, what have been its financial consequences, its effects on retirement patterns, its impact on retention of highly productive faculty, and its effect on staffing levels?
- Has the institution considered alternatives to tenure, such as a system of contracts? If so, what has been the effect of the policy on hiring, renewal, termination, and replacement?

Tenure Process and Procedures

The governing board should be willing to actively review the processes and procedures by which the institution makes decisions on appointment, reappointment, and tenure. At stake is an institution's ability to fulfill its mission, treat individuals fairly, and reach its strategic objectives. As the institution's final legal authority, the board also has a clear interest in ensuring that the procedures work as described. Ineffective policies or slipshod procedures can embroil institutional leaders and boards in painful and expensive controversies.

If a board ever doubts whether it should exercise active oversight of academic personnel policies, all it takes is one difficult lawsuit to drive the point home, especially a suit in which the trustees are named personally. Although litigation has become common throughout higher education, there are ways to minimize the likelihood of legal challenges. In developing and implementing the institution's policies, leaders should keep two goals paramount: Individuals must be treated fairly, and the institution's mission, goals, and authority must be honored. How is this to happen?

Trustees will want to ask a number of questions, many of which will be placed in context in the following section:

DATA POINT

47% of respondents said it is moderately or very important to establish alternatives to tenure.

50% said it is not important.

- Have the faculty and the administration worked collaboratively to develop the institution's policies and procedures?
- Has expert legal counsel, experienced in college and university law, carefully reviewed the proposed policies and procedures?
- Has the board been informed of the reasons for proposed significant changes in policies and procedures? Has it been given the opportunity to raise questions and make comments prior to being asked to act?

Faculty guides and handbooks defining tenure and other faculty employment policies, as well as the major processes and procedures related to them, have the force of a contract. For this reason, trustees must be assured that scrupulous care has been given to the formation of these policies. Institutions bind themselves legally by their own policies and procedures, and they are measured against the commitments they have made.

The president, academic officers, and the institution's counsel should describe clearly to new trustees the inner workings of the faculty personnel system. In the standard doctrine that most institutions have adopted, for example, tenure is a permanent appointment that a faculty member gains by successfully completing a probationary period and subsequently being reappointed at its conclusion. Technically, the decisions made by the institution in the penultimate year of service determine whether the person will be allowed to serve long enough to gain a tenured appointment. Although this may appear to be a fine point, it has important implications for the ways in which procedures are implemented and notification is provided to a faculty member when an appointment is not renewed.

Many institutions have developed a series of best practices in the arena of faculty policies and procedures. A quick review of these will give trustees a base of information as they exercise their responsibilities to review and assess the policies of their own institutions. Again, circumstances and traditions produce a variety of valid practices.

- *The provisional period.* Although seven years is the standard provisional period, institutions are free to set longer or shorter periods. Agreements about when an individual will be considered for tenure must be in writing, especially if there are variations in the provisional period relating to prior service at another institution or because of other circumstances. Thus, once the clock begins to tick for tenure, any interruptions in the provisional period (for example, through illness or special leave for childbirth) must be defined in writing and agreed to by both parties.
- *Nature of appointments.* During the provisional period, individuals are evaluated annually for renewal for appointments normally made for one year, with no right or expectancy of renewal. Persons who are not to be eligible for tenure should be clearly informed about the nature of the appointment, and unless the institution has developed explicit policies to the contrary, they cannot be allowed to serve beyond the conclusion of the provisional period.
- *Feedback.* Clear feedback should be given during the provisional period. From time to time, a written summary should address a person's performance in teaching, scholarship, and service. Those preparing communications, typically a dean or a

department chair, will know that their goal is to provide general information that is useful to evaluate an individual's service, without in any way suggesting future commitments or decisions on the part of the institution.

- *Mid-service review.* At least once during the provisional period, there should be an extensive evaluation of the candidate's work, followed by a conference with the department chair and/or dean. The review should indicate clearly the person's areas of strength and weakness and the steps needed to strengthen performance. At this point in the provisional period, many candidates come to understand that the appointment may not represent a long-term match with the institution.

- *Tenure file or portfolio.* As part of being considered for tenure, faculty members in most institutions prepare elaborate tenure files or portfolios that adhere to a prescribed set of definitions and deadlines. The individual's materials normally include a detailed curriculum vita, results of teaching evaluations, copies of course syllabi and publications, and a candidate's statements about teaching and research. The department chair often will obtain individual evaluations of teaching by former students and peers, as well as recommendations from experts in the candidate's field inside and outside the institution. If any variations are granted in the review schedule, others under simultaneous review should be given the same opportunities. Although most of the materials will be submitted in confidence, everyone should be aware that legal or regulatory challenges could mean that the information becomes part of a public record. In such instances, it may be difficult to protect the names of recommenders or reviewers. Because of this, some institutions have adopted policies that allow candidates access to their files.

- *Levels of recommendation.* Depending on the institution, a departmental committee or the tenured faculty of the department will read and discuss the materials and make a recommendation to the department chair. The chair may make a separate recommendation or join with the department's. In a university, the department's recommendation usually passes on to a review committee composed of elected faculty in the school or the college in which the department is located. The recommendation then moves to the dean of the college and then to the chief academic officer (sometimes preceded by a universitywide committee in large institutions). Finally, the recommendations come to the president, who makes a decision or prepares a recommendation for the academic affairs committee of the board.

- *Peer review.* At the heart of the complex system of faculty appointment and tenure is the phenomenon of peer review. Faculty members at the department level believe they are in the best position to evaluate the work of a colleague. Some or many of them have been trained in the same discipline and know best the person's teaching and scholarship. If the department is unanimous and has strong confidence in a recommendation, then it is likely that each of the subsequent levels of review will agree, and in the vast majority of cases tenure is granted. If a department's strong recommendation is not accepted at other levels, an explosion of criticism often reverberates throughout the campus. In the academic world, when a department's decision has been rejected it is an affront to its professional judgment.

- *Administrative review.* At administrative levels of review, several examinations occur. One relates to the quality of the individual, another to questions of need and strategic fit, and yet another to compliance with institutional policies and procedures. Cases should not move forward if any flaws exist in the way the case has been considered. Allegations of bias or suspect considerations in the review must be addressed before the process continues.

- *Grievance procedures.* Most institutions provide several levels of grievance redress. One of these principally regards questions of procedural adequacy, as distinguished from substantive judgment. Other grievance procedures are available if a person who is denied tenure can establish a *prima facie* case of discrimination or violation of academic freedom. In such instances, the review will be more elaborate, because it must discover whether unwritten and indefensible reasons exist for the decision. The chance to bring a grievance is an important part of due-process procedures in public and private colleges and universities.

Trustees will find that most of the problems that arise in tenure cases relate to split votes at the department level. These cases often lead to a weak positive or a negative recommendation at higher peer levels of review and frequently to rejection by the dean, provost, and president. If the department is split but still offers a positive recommendation, it either may be a way to save a colleague from embarrassment or a way to pass along an unpleasant case to the next level. Frequently, cases of this type create problems for the institution because individuals may be encouraged by some colleagues to seek redress for the decision. Faculty members who have experienced negative judgments frequently are counseled by attorneys or organizations that respresent faculty to pursue the case through all of the existing grievance procedures and to consider every legal avenue.

One of the important issues for trustees is whether the institution's standards for tenure and promotion adequately reflect its purposes and strategic goals. Nothing is more significant in shaping an institution's identity, character, and achievements than its permanent faculty members. Boards will want to monitor whether the espoused goals in research and teaching are exemplified in promotion and tenure decisions. Trustees also should press the question of whether the field of the person being tenured has sufficient centrality and demand from students to represent a wise strategic investment of permanent funds.

The issue of standards always is present in the relative weight given to effectiveness in teaching and research. For example, trustees may ask whether the institution has differentiated its expectations for scholarship according to its mission. In *Scholarship Reconsidered*, Ernest Boyer wrote that the true coin of the realm in most universities is the scholarship of discovery.[12] That is to say, only work that posits original arguments or findings possesses significant value for tenure and promotion.

In fact, most faculty members, because of their other duties and teaching commitments, are much more likely to be involved in what Boyer calls the scholarship of integration or interpretation. In work of this kind, scholars are analyzing and synthesizing the significance of the literature on a certain topic. Other faculty members are focused on applied scholarship, bringing the findings of a field of abstract knowledge into the world of practice. Boyer concludes that the standards for faculty evaluation should be more sensitive to the scholarship of teaching and to the continuing research and study an instructor must perform to stay current in the field and be effective in the classroom.

Boyer's analysis touched a nerve among faculty, reflecting the widespread feeling that standards for tenure, promotion, and salary increases often were unclear or unfair. Nonetheless, his categories give trustees an opportunity to reflect on the critical question of the alignment between institutional goals and the actual process of faculty evaluation. The need for a person's scholarship to undergo peer review is essential, but many faculty members feel thwarted by the rigidity with which research expectations are limited to publication in a handful of peer-reviewed journals. Trustees need not enter into the endless debates about the nature of peer review, but they can helpfully focus the discussion on whether the standards embedded in the tenure and promotion process embody the institution's values.

Promotion

Institutions handle promotion in a variety of ways. In many cases, faculty members must serve a minimum period before they are eligible for promotion to the subsequent rank, although in some institutions length of time at rank is irrelevant. In most institutions, the tenure-granting decision comes with a promotion in rank to associate professor, although the practice is not uniform.

To cut to the heart of the issue, trustees might ask members of the administration and faculty how they regard a promotion to full professor. Is the process a stringent one? What does the promotion to that rank really mean? Is promotion something that becomes increasingly likely the longer a person serves? Trustees would do well to ask the chief academic officer and/or the deans to provide information on the average period of service at the rank of associate professor prior to appointment to full professor. They will learn that the variations are enormous between various schools and fields. Discussion of these differences is helpful for understanding the dynamics of faculty evaluation and professional expectation.

Faculty Development

Faculty members often spend their entire careers at one or two institutions. As time passes, they may shift the focus of their teaching and research interests and, in some cases, develop entirely new approaches to their work. The wider world of ideas also is constantly changing. New fields open up, innovative methods of teaching are developed, and whole new ways of transmitting and analyzing information become available through new technologies.

How do academic professionals keep up with these changes? The term "faculty development" commonly describes the effort to provide faculty with the means to keep abreast of changes in teaching, learning, and their disciplines. In many ways, traditional programs such as sabbatical leaves and professional travel are part of the effort to provide opportunities for professional renewal. Most campuses also have developed efforts to assist faculty members in developing new courses and pedagogies, including greater use of technology. Through variously named "teaching centers," faculty and staff sponsor seminars and programs in which they share ideas about teaching, invite experts to the campus, and collect and provide information about trends in teaching and learning.

The logic of trustee support for programs of faculty development is persuasive. Institutions of higher learning can only be as effective as the quality of their faculty, so investments to enhance their work represent funds well spent. In reviewing policies and programs related to the faculty, trustees will want to know the status of the faculty-development program and to ensure that the institution has effective ways to assist faculty with professional renewal. Considering the following questions may be helpful:

DATA POINT

83% of respondents said faculty development programs are moderately or very important. **46%** said programs designed to enhance faculty use of technology in teaching are very important. **37%** said programs designed to support faculty in different career stages are very important.

- What is the scope of programs and staffing of the "teaching center" and of related activities and seminars to improve teaching?
- What programs are available to assist faculty in the use of technology?
- What policies are in place concerning professional travel, and how do faculty use the funds?
- Is there support for faculty members to attend meetings on topics in teaching methods or curricular development?
- What are the institution's sabbatical-leave and released-time policies, and how do they relate to mission and to strategic objectives?

Statistical Profile of the Faculty

Trustees can increase their understanding of many crucial issues in faculty personnel policies if they are provided with a statistical profile that displays faculty appointment, tenure, and promotion patterns. Trustees do not need the elaborate level of detail important to administrators, but there should be regular times each academic year when the whole board is given summary data. Good data tell a story.

Trustees should expect data that reveal the number and the percentage of faculty members who hold tenure, those eligible and not eligible for tenure, and numbers of adjunct or part-time positions, all differentiated according to departments, divisions, and schools.

Trustees should receive information on the pattern and probability of individuals receiving tenure related both to measures of probability defined by the cohort of faculty with whom the candidates entered the institution, as well as according to results during the actual year of the tenure decision. Findings related to departmental and school patterns should be brought to the board's attention.

The board should be given information derived from statistical profiles that can be used to construct projection models to indicate the anticipated levels and percentages of future tenure appointments, assuming that tenure probabilities continue in the future as they have unfolded in the past. The tenure model obviously should produce projections with various assumptions.

Trustees should have the breakdown of faculty members by gender and ethnicity and their patterns in tenure and rank. Although affirmative action has become a highly variable process, depending on the legislative and legal jurisdiction of an institution, there continues to be a shared awareness in higher education that diverse faculty interests and backgrounds constitute strength in preparing students educationally and socially.

Trustees need data on faculty salaries presented by rank and discipline or by clusters of disciplines, along with benchmark data at comparable institutions. This information helps define the institution's competitive strategic position. Trustees should receive summary information and measures concerning the teaching and research loads of the faculty by college, school, or division. The data should indicate average number of students taught, other student contact hours, and time allocated for research. Faculty research achievements and service commitments should be summarized in ways that are comprehensible to trustees.

Monitoring Faculty Policies and Procedures

The foregoing analysis of faculty policies and procedures provides board members with a perspective to inform their efforts to monitor and evaluate procedures for tenure and contract renewal. The trustee voice sounds several different notes along the register of its authority. At one point, it promises compliance with best practices and with legal, contractual, regulatory, and (perhaps) institutional requirements. At another point, it pledges commitments to the values of fairness and integrity. At yet another, it presses for the alignment of the institution's standards and aspirations with decisions in specific cases. The governing board plays a pivotal role in ensuring the effectiveness of these crucial policies by providing the final review.

> **DATA POINT**
>
> **37%** of respondents said it is very important to hire more women and minority faculty. (In 1984, the figure was **23%**.) **53%** from publics said such plans are very important, compared with **33%** from privates.

What insights, perspectives, and questions will board members want to bring to the exercise of this important responsibility?

- ***Clarity and coherence.*** The various deadlines, stages, and components in the process must be clearly, consistently, and coherently defined and connected to one another. The board should be assured that this is the case and should spot-check documents to see that the language is clear and accurate.

- ***Differentiated authority.*** The role and authority of each separate level in the decision-making process should be defined. Faculty committees, for example, have the authority to recommend, not to enact decisions, as does each level prior to the designated final authority, typically the board. The evidence used in decisions, such as student evaluations, is always subject to interpretation by professional judgment. Have these points been made clear?

- ***Fairness to individuals.*** The board should be sure that individuals receive timely information about the nature of the process and advice about how to follow each provision in the review procedure. Information and expectations concerning performance should be communicated periodically, and the candidate should be able to address any areas of concern. Boards should ask how the procedures guarantee fairness to the individual. Sound grievance procedures not only protect the individual but help keep controversial cases out of the courts.

- ***Integrity.*** The board should be sure that tenure and appointment procedures clearly affirm such fundamental values as high standards, academic freedom, and equal opportunity. Trustees should ask questions and examine documents to see whether procedures are built into the review process to protect against invidious discrimination or the violation of academic freedom.

- ***High standards.*** The board should be aware of how performance standards are articulated and applied. An institution's standards should reflect its mission and strategic commitments, and they must be applied consistently and rigorously. To claim to have standards but to fail to determine decisions consistently opens the institution to a host of problems, including charges of discrimination. Similarly situated individuals must be assessed by the same criteria in actual practice, regardless of abstract statements.

- ***Risk management.*** Board members must be aware that flaws in procedures for tenure and reappointment carry major risks of internal conflict and legal action that can lead to substantial reputational and financial risks. The board needs to be assured that those involved in tenure decisions at each level understand and comply with the process and that legal counsel is satisfied with all procedures.

[1] Berberet, William G., and Linda McMillin. "The American Professoriate in Transition." *AGB Priorities*, No. 18 (Spring 2002).

[2] The American Association for Higher Education (AAHE) has a continuing project including conferences, special studies, and publications on faculty roles and responsibilities. See *The New Pathways Working Paper Series* from AAHE. There also is a large-scale continuing study of faculty appointment and tenure policies and practices at the Harvard University Graduate School of Education supported by the Pew Charitable Trusts. Various reports and books are available through the project.

[3] American Association of University Professors. *1940 Statement of Principles and Interpretive Comments on Academic Freedom and Tenure*. Washington, D.C.: American Association of University Professors, 1984.

[4] For a collection of essays providing support for tenure, see *The Case for Tenure*, Matthew Finkin, ed. Ithaca, N.Y.: Cornell University Press, 1996.

[5] Morrill, Richard L. and Edward D. Eddy, "Living with Tenure Without Quotas." *Liberal Education*, Vol. 61, no. 3 (October 1975), pages 399-417.

[6] Baldwin, Roger G., and Jay L. Chronister. *Teaching Without Tenure: Policies and Practices for a New Era*. Baltimore: Johns Hopkins University Press, 2001. This work provides a full analysis of temporary appointments.

[7] Benjamin, Ernst. "Part-Time Faculty, Full-Time Concerns." *Trusteeship*, Vol. 8, no. 4 (July/August 2000), pages 13-16.

[8] Licata, Christine M. "Precepts for Post-Tenure Reviews." *Trusteeship*, Vol. 7, no. 6 (November/December 1999), pages 8-13. This article parallels the argument here and provides additional information about tenure reviews.

[9] Baldwin, Roger G., and Jay L. Chronister. *Teaching Without Tenure: Policies and Practices for a New Era*. Baltimore: Johns Hopkins University Press, 2001.

[10] For a fuller treatment of issues and opportunities in early retirement see Ehrenberg, Ronald G. "Don't Shy Away From Retirement Questions." *Trusteeship*, Vol. 9, no. 4 (July/August 2001), pages 8-13.

[11] Chait, Richard P. "The Future of Academic Tenure." *AGB Priorities*, No. 3 (Spring 1995).

[12] Boyer, Ernest L. *Scholarship Reconsidered: Priorities of the Professoriate*. Princeton, N.J.: Carnegie Foundation for the Advancement of Teaching, 1990.

CHAPTER 7

The Academic Affairs Committee

To carry out the wide and complex range of responsibilities concerning academic matters, governing boards normally rely on a committee on academic affairs. Known by many different titles, structured in varying ways, and charged with an array of duties in different institutions, the committee's primary responsibilities include academic and faculty matters.

A typical private-institution board of 20-40 members is too large to process extensive information about the educational program and to deliberate in depth about specific issues. To be effective, the board has to rely on the work conducted in committee. If the committee is well informed, sensitive to its special role, and has good leadership and an effective internal dynamic, it can make a substantial contribution to the board and to the effectiveness of the whole institution. In some cases, small boards may function as a committee of the whole for educational issues, but in doing so its members will need to be aware of their special decision-making role in the academic sphere. That may be a tall order, given the board's many other responsibilities.

Whatever its specific set of duties, the academic affairs committee can serve as a mechanism that unifies the total work of the board. Because it focuses on the defining purposes of the institution, the committee can integrate the board's role in collaborative strategic leadership. In the academic affairs committee, trustees, administrators, and faculty members together can discuss the educational values and academic programs that provide the animating center for all the administrative and financial issues that normally crowd the board's agenda.[1]

DATA POINT

50% of respondents said the work of their board's academic affairs committee includes academic and faculty issues only.

20% said the committee's work also includes enrollment management and student services.

The Work of the Committee

If the committee is to provide the board with an integrative perspective, it will need to find effective and efficient ways to fulfill its duties. First, this means establishing a productive working relationship between the committee and an administrative counterpart, usually the chief academic officer. This person can be expected to enjoy the full confidence of the president, who periodically will work with the committee's administrative coordinator to build agendas around action items and broad strategic issues.

Working with the committee chair, the chief academic officer should develop an information calendar that defines the assessment data and statistical reports that will be presented at each meeting on a rotating basis. A fall meeting might be the time, say, for presenting the statistical faculty profile, and a spring meeting the time for sharing the results of program reviews. By rotating information at set meetings, committee members can anticipate and analyze information within a familiar framework. Over time, this helps them see trends, deepen their understanding, and sharpen their questions. Though all board members should receive summaries of important data, the committee should be given more detailed information and special studies.

One of the principal tasks of the committee is to decide what to report as information and what to recommend for action to the board. The impact of its reports will be greatest if the committee has thought carefully about the purposes of its own deliberations. If the committee consciously monitors and assesses the academic program in a strategic framework, it can bring to life issues that otherwise appear to be inconsequential. To achieve this aim, the committee's administrative coordinator will want to illuminate the information provided to the committee, indicating what can and cannot be learned from it. "Reading" data strategically is not a passive task but one that leads to further inquiries, comparative analyses, and the pursuit of explanations for troubling or unexpected indicators.

In turn, the committee will think hard about creative and effective ways to report its insights and findings to educate the board about issues that eventually may come forward for action. To do so, it may focus a brief report on a key issue at each full board meeting, providing a few charts to show trends in areas such as retention, tenure patterns, or admissions rates to graduate school.

The committee's effort to interpret information has the ultimate goal of discerning what plans and actions can be designed to improve performance. The committee should expect reports from the administration or faculty to suggest specific actions to meet goals related to raising educational quality. Where this orientation is lacking, the committee can communicate through its questions and comments that it expects the loop to be closed between knowing and doing, between evaluating and enacting. Trustee monitoring and evaluation can energize the academic decision-making process, fueling collaboration among the board, administration, and faculty while driving strategy toward implementation. Because the committee's work involves continuing face-to-face relationships, the board's monitoring and evaluating activities are likely to influence the agendas of administrators and faculty members. The committee thus holds one of the keys to ensuring the institution meets its objectives.

What happens when problems and challenges come to the committee's attention? How does it translate its authority into effective action? After all, it is the administration and the faculty who have the primary responsibility to assess and improve programs, while the board simply reviews that process. It would be a fundamental mistake to shift the administrative dimensions of evaluation to the board, which would be ineffective in that role. Yet by demanding accountability and assessing performance, the board has a powerful mechanism to foster change.

To illustrate how an academic affairs committee might respond to problems through its monitoring of the academic program, the following hypothetical case study might be helpful. It illustrates how an academic affairs committee might do its work and examines how the committee and the board itself might address an academic problem through measured and collaborative action. The underlying question is whether the governing board, working through its academic affairs committee, can make a difference in the academic program without interfering with the professional prerogatives of the faculty or administration.

Case 3: Problems in Academic Advising at a Regional State University

A state university with a strong regional reputation and an enrollment of 10,000 full-time and 4,000 part-time students has approved a strategic plan based on a vision to be a student-centered university with a strong focus on applied research in fields where it can become a national leader. Consistent with the vision is a strong new emphasis on the academic advising of students through a reorganized and reenergized system focused on faculty involvement.

In reviewing summary data on a student satisfaction survey, a member of the academic affairs committee notes an apparent problem with student advising in one of the university's schools. At a committee meeting, he asks the provost to find out whether the problem is real. The provost indicates he is unaware of any special problems but will report back to the committee.

It turns out that the detailed information troubles the committee. It reveals that a large proportion of students in the school, more than 40 percent, believe it is "difficult" or "impossible" to make an appointment with their faculty adviser. Other aspects of advising in the survey also receive low ratings. The dean reports that the problem seems to be centered on three of the six departments. He claims the issue may be overblown because many students expect to make instant or same-day contact with an adviser and refuse to plan ahead. The provost notes, however, that no other schools or departments in the university have the same rate of negative responses on the item, so the difference is significant. He tells the committee he is concerned that the dean was not more forthcoming initially about the issue given its strategic importance, but that the dean has volunteered to discuss the problem with the chairs of the three departments.

Several members of the committee are uncomfortable with the situation. They suggest that the renewed emphasis on advising is a crucial aspect of the strategic plan, that the results are worrisome in themselves, and that they send a terrible message that academic administration is still "business as usual." They wonder whether the provost would find it appropriate to receive a resolution from the committee requesting the dean to prepare a report on specific actions the school intends to take to meet the strategic goals of the advising plan. The provost understands the significance of the issue but is undecided whether this is a wise step, because it may be interpreted as a signal that the board lacks confidence in his leadership. Because the school in question has a high volume of funded research, faculty members may see this as the board meddling with the way they establish their priorities and set their schedules. He asks that the president discuss the issue with the committee.

After a full discussion, the president indicates that under these circumstances the committee's approach is appropriate. She tells the committee that she has no objection to the committee's officially requesting a follow-up report that would, in effect, charge the provost to communicate the committee's expectations to the dean. The committee's action does not require a formal resolution of the whole board but will be part of the chair's oral report as a matter that is under consideration.

In explaining her reasons for accepting the committee's idea, the president suggests that this type of action will not undercut the provost's responsibility. The board committee collaborated with the administration, acted through it, and examined the facts before making a decision. It did not prescribe or impose a solution. Because the board recently had endorsed the strategic plan that several committee members helped create, it would be dangerous to invite their participation, give them information, ask for their questions and concerns, and then deflect their request for a report. As the institution's final authority, the board can send a powerful symbolic message of accountability because the request is tied to a goal that everyone, including the faculty senate, has endorsed. The committee's action shows it intends to use its authority within a balanced process of shared leadership.

One can easily imagine other scenarios under different presidents. Some presidents would argue that a board committee that directs the provost to take a specific action sets a dangerous precedent and undermines the authority of both the president and the provost. In this interpretation, the board committee's action, although innocent in itself, turns committee members into academic executives and implies that the board can act directly without going through the president. Presidents of this mind might suggest that the board's concerns should be honored, but that it is up to the president to tell the provost to seek corrective action at the school and departmental level and to report to the president on it, and he in turn to the board.

Readers will want to consider questions of their own regarding this case. Does it matter how this kind of issue is handled? Is the academic affairs committee's active role appropriate? Has it become too involved in faculty matters? Which of the presidential responses

---

DATA POINT

76% of respondents said it is important for the board to have a significant voice in the nature and shape of academic programs.

20% said it was not important.

is persuasive? How should one come to a judgment about these matters?

The case raises several issues about the way academic affairs committees should function. The first has to do with local judgments of the legitimacy of the committee's action. Standing agreements, traditions, settled expectations, and the values of the campus culture will answer the question of legitimacy in different ways for each institution. It is vital that the board committee act within broad patterns of perceived legitimacy. Under the right circumstances, the limits of legitimacy can justifiably be stretched but not broken, unless for very good reasons.

The second issue concerns the committee's fundamental goal. The academic affairs committee can be flexible in its methods, but its aim is to be an active partner in a collaborative process of educational decision making. The committee's purpose is not to use its authority as an end in itself; rather, it is to create a zone of accountability within which those responsible must answer for reaching the educational goals they have set for themselves. For this reason, the committee raises questions, makes evaluations, and asks for demonstrable results. As it does so, it may indeed be signaling that the administration's or the faculty's responses have been passive or ineffective, but it must do so in a way that respects each participant's contribution to the decision-making process.

Program Approval

In approving new programs or discontinuing existing ones, it is again the work of the committee that determines the recommendation that will flow to the whole board. Scrutiny of the process that has produced a recommendation for a new program is the committee's responsibility, as is the final assessment of issues related to strategic fit, academic quality, student demand, and financing. The board relies on the verification provided through the committee that a new program passes the tests of procedure and of substance. When the committee recommends that programs be discontinued, again the committee must review the case in detail and ensure that all parties have been fully heard.

An area in which the approval of a new academic offering has become challenging for academic affairs committees concerns programs requested by donors and corporations. Faculty often fear that donors or corporations will try to control the curriculum, hold sway on personnel decisions, or short-circuit normal governance patterns. In such cases, the committee can play a crucial monitoring role, providing a forum for opposing views and drawing lines to protect institutional integrity. Even though academic affairs commit-

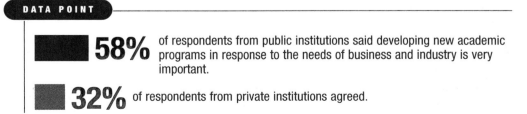

DATA POINT

58% of respondents from public institutions said developing new academic programs in response to the needs of business and industry is very important.

32% of respondents from private institutions agreed.

tees and boards have the authority to create new ventures without prior faculty approval, doing so would be wise only in unusual circumstances.

If a controversy arises over a proposed program, the academic affairs committee can make a valuable contribution by inviting, with the administration's approval, faculty leaders who oppose the program to present their views directly to the committee. In controversial cases surrounding major gifts or corporate support for new programs, the administration usually is seen as already committed to the venture and may no longer be perceived as neutral. The committee can place the issue in a new light by reviewing the issues evenhandedly and displaying concern for the strategic dimension of the problem and the integrity of the decision-making process. Enough institutions have experienced problems in these spheres to suggest that the active involvement of the board committee can be an appropriate safeguard. The committee ordinarily should be able to keep proposals on the normal track for full review and approval.

Faculty Personnel Policies and Decisions

Although legal counsel, the administration, and faculty committees will carry the heaviest weight in developing and recommending major faculty employment policies and procedures, only the board can finalize them. Drawing on valuable perspectives from other walks of life, the members of the academic affairs committee will want to study and critique these policies and procedures.

As the institution stakes its reputation on commitments to such values as fairness, equal opportunity, high standards, consistency, and academic freedom, these values must be translated into all faculty employment policies and practices. The academic affairs committee guarantees the accuracy of the translation.

There are substantial variations among institutions in the way trustees are involved in decisions about faculty appointments, promotion, and tenure. Along the spectrum from small to large institutions, the trustee role reduces to a formality or even disappears. In tenure decisions, the stakes are high, and trustee involvement can be momentous. The academic affairs committee should not be asked to provide a more authoritative judgment than a committee of faculty peers about a candidate's qualifications. The campus would suffer a crisis of confidence if a committee of lay trustees were to substitute its judgment for that of prior levels of review, including that of the administration, on the merits of a tenure case. Such a decision also might violate the spirit or the letter of the institution's policies. The committee's work normally does not extend to studying tenure portfolios; rather, it is limited to ensuring that the tenure policies and procedures of the institution are functioning as intended.

Ironically, to make an informed judgment about policy and procedure, the committee will need to observe the application of criteria in specific cases. A brief summary of the professional qualifications of candidates and of recommendations made in prior stages of the review process will contain important information for the committee. Based on this information, committee members will be able to make observations or ask questions about whether decisions are consistent with stated expectations, institutional mission, and strategic aspirations.

From the profiles of candidates and the statistical faculty profile it has received, the committee will be able to note trends in faculty achievements in teaching and scholarship, academic backgrounds, and ethnic representation. The nature and future of the institution, including its financial future, are largely being defined through these decisions, so the committee's review constitutes a prime example of the power of attentive and active questioning. What is the precise nature of the scholarship of the candidate being accepted for tenure, and how does it differ from those being rejected? How do the institution's claims about the role of teaching translate into tenure decisions? Are standards consistent at the various levels of review? What explains divergent decisions by the dean and the department? Have all procedures relating to fairness and equal opportunity been scrupulously applied?

Should the committee's review raise serious concerns, members have the option to examine information in greater detail, even to read a full tenure file. In doing so, the aim, again, is not to second-guess the professional judgment of others but to be assured that practices and procedures are fully in accord with policy. The committee's occasional study of the details of a case can contribute to a more rigorous and consistent process.

If arbitrary or unfair decisions emerge, the consequences will be turmoil that can become crippling, especially at the department level. If, on the other hand, the board is confident that procedures are being fairly and consistently applied and that high standards reflect the institution's identity and aspirations, the committee and the board will be able to provide steady support to those making tough decisions. Tenure decisions register only as yes or no, up or out. They are total and final, unlike promotion or salary decisions that can be calibrated or revisited. Moreover, because such decisions may diminish or even close future professional opportunities, they are fraught with emotion. Personal and public attacks may come, and in their wake may be lawsuits. Since little can be said publicly about personnel matters, it can be a lonely and difficult time for those who have made the key decisions. The board should understand these circumstances and support those who carry the largest burdens in the decision, typically department chairs, deans, vice presidents, and the president.

Another reason the academic affairs committee will want to review tenure decisions as to process and pattern is to be aware of problems and controversies that may emerge on campus, in the press, or in the courts. Board members, like anyone else, always handle bad news and controversy better when they are prepared.

Depending on the size and protocols of the institution, the academic affairs committee may submit a report to the full board on tenure for its information and, depending on the institution, for its action. Only after the board has acted can candidates be notified of the tenure decision.

Committee Membership

To fulfill the academic affairs committee's potential as a vital strategic-monitoring and decision-making body, the committee's membership will need to be carefully considered. The selection of a committee chair is especially important. This trustee will need to interact effectively in many relationships—with other board members, the president and other top administrators, faculty members, and students. The chair should have the stature to inspire respect in all these individuals. He or she will need to demonstrate a clear commitment to the centrality of the academic program in institutional decisions and a deep interest in educational questions. Because committee deliberations often involve sensitive personnel questions, campus controversies, or disputes over governance authority, the chair typically is someone who is circumspect and knows institutional policies well. A requisite skill is knowing how to interpret the decision-making system to others.

The chair also should be a key participant in other committees and task forces that are involved in strategic planning. Committee schedules may make overlapping memberships difficult, but careful planning will make it possible. The aim is to achieve linkage among committees reflecting the integrative nature of most of the institution's important decisions. In addition, the board might want a member or two of the academic affairs committee to serve on other key committees, especially finance. The committee's connection to financial matters is essential for reviewing the implementation of academic priorities.

Most boards have faculty members serving as members or observers on board committees, and this is especially helpful for academic affairs. To be sure, the faculty members must not speak for colleagues whose views they do not know, so the faculty participants need to exercise care in how and what they communicate to the committee. If the committee makes specific recommendations on personnel matters, such as individual tenure cases, faculty members should absent themselves to protect against any perceived or real conflicts of interest.

Many institutions seek to have at least one individual on the committee who is a professional in higher education—a president, dean, or distinguished faculty member of another institution. Such a person can make a substantial contribution. Deliberations on most issues begin with establishing context, and academicians can provide credible insights. Problem-solving skills and sensitivities honed in a similar environment elsewhere often are beneficial to the committee, especially in helping other board members understand the intricacies of the academic culture.

Because the effectiveness of the committee depends on its members being informed about broad educational issues, the institution might wish to provide subscriptions for committee members to higher education periodicals. *Change* and *Liberal Education* magazines focus on

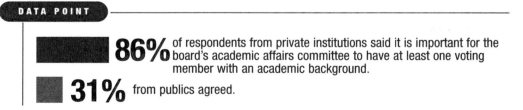

DATA POINT

86% of respondents from private institutions said it is important for the board's academic affairs committee to have at least one voting member with an academic background.

31% from publics agreed.

trends in teaching and learning, and AGB's *Trusteeship* addresses educational issues from the perspective of a board member. The *Chronicle of Higher Education* is a useful comprehensive weekly news source but demands more time than most board members have available. An efficient approach is for the committee's administrative liaison to circulate key articles and opinion pieces, especially on topics the committee is considering.

Some boards ask students to participate in committee meetings, sometimes as members. Many boards do not. The burden on students to participate can be considerable, so devoting time and energy to orient them to their assignments is essential. The personal experience of students in campus life and academic programs gives them the chance to offer a fresh and personal view that trustees may find valuable. Most students chosen for the task of committee service will be top performers, often enchanting trustees by their enthusiasm and achievements. There always are exceptions, but most students can be trusted to speak only for themselves and to avoid politicized issues. Again, as with faculty representatives, students should excuse themselves from deliberations or votes on specific tenure cases.

The work of the academic affairs committee will be more effective if its members periodically attend campus events—lectures, concerts, programs—to experience the campus in action. Although some presidents discourage informal contact between the board and the campus community, fearing back-channel communications, members of the academic affairs committee will want to experience campus life directly. Social events and dinners surrounding board and committee meetings represent a good opportunity for committee members to know one another personally, and brief presentations at committee meetings by faculty and staff help trustees better understand the institution.

Reflecting both the nature of the issues with which it deals and the expertise of committee members, many board committees have a partially scripted role. As a large part of their work, committees on finance, audit, facilities, and investment apply rules, standards, and expectations that follow a prescribed pattern. Clearly, this is far from the case in academic affairs, where there are far fewer controlling expectations. These circumstances present the academic affairs committee with an opportunity to contribute decisively to the effectiveness of the institution.

In various ways, academic affairs committees can become important links in the chain of strategic decision making and evaluation that institutions use to design and implement their academic futures. If the committee does not have a meaningful effect on this total process, then neither will the board itself. That is why the chief executive and board leaders should reflect carefully and creatively about the responsibilities, membership, and workings of the academic affairs committee.

---

[1] For ideas that parallel and supplement this chapter, see: Wood, Richard J. "Academic Affairs Committee." *AGB Board Basics Series.* Washington, D.C.: Association of Governing Boards of Universities and Colleges, 1997.

Conclusion

In their illuminating study, *The Effective Board of Trustees*, Richard P. Chait, Thomas P. Holland, and Barbara E. Taylor recount the contrasting responses of two different governing boards to proposals for curricular change. In the first instance, the faculty of a denominational college decided to eliminate the requirement for Bible courses, triggering the board's concern. As one trustee recalled:

"We were shocked by the faculty's announcement that they had decided to eliminate these requirements. Since it was founded by the denomination, courses in Bible have always been important for our students. We decided not to act hastily, to take some time to consider the issue. The president helped us to put the issue into the framework of the mission of the college.... I think we're coming together on some compromises that will be acceptable to almost everyone." [1]

The president affirmed the board's role:

"The board was opposed to the elimination of Bible courses. To their credit, they challenged the faculty to show how the curriculum could meet the mission of the college, as set forth in the mission statement, without this component."

The authors cite the president's and the board's actions as examples of trustee effectiveness because they placed the decision squarely within the context of the institution's mission and heritage.

The second incident reveals a different approach, relating to the discontinuation of an astronomy program because of high costs and small enrollments. One trustee commented on the decision:

"You have to understand that this event, dropping astronomy, is like MIT dropping engineering.... No one on the board saw the market for the program. It was a financial decision.... Despite sentiment, despite the fact that the college's first president was an astronomer and that we had an observatory and a field station, the board stood its ground."

The authors do not make a judgment about whether this board made the right decision for the long term. For them, the problem is the way the decision was made, with no searching consideration of its implications for mission, image, and heritage. The decision is reduced to financial questions alone. As that criterion takes hold on a campus, programs are invented or abandoned strictly to fit market needs, with little sense of their integration with institutional purpose, tradition, and distinctiveness. According to the authors, it fits a pattern of decision making used by less effective boards.

The Effective Board of Trustees outlines a portrait of trustee effectiveness that in many ways parallels the concepts and strategies proposed in this text. The authors are concerned, however, with the full range of board decision making, not just academic affairs. Yet they emphasize that effective boards (as known through reputation and as associated with financial and other indicators of strength) are highly conscious of institutional distinctiveness and values, as well as of the importance of being well informed about the institution and the academic profession. The authors also stress that effective boards need an analytical perspective, political sensitivity to other stakeholders, and a strategic orientation to decision making.

As the foregoing examples suggest, academic institutions are distinctive organizations that must carefully balance the ways they make decisions, especially in the academic sphere. Colleges and universities must synthesize the educational ideals embedded in their identities with the realities of organizational life.

The integration of these inescapable tensions is best achieved through a strategic approach to decision making. As trustees set their academic responsibilities in this framework, educational issues convey the institution's story. The board's role is clarified, and its work is invigorated. In the strategic context, otherwise static claims about mission become the basis for enacting distinctive programs. Mute institutional facts speak with meaning. Budgets embody plans. Random activity becomes goal-directed. Environmental trends become challenges and opportunities. Evaluations trigger processes of self-improvement. Unclear expectations become clear responsibilities. And in the process, the board's authority becomes a pivotal aspect of collaborative leadership.

The board's role in academic affairs is that of an active and influential partner in a continuing dialogue, but the board's is not the voice that dominates the conversation. Programs, proposals, and recommendations are first voiced by others, and the board is an active listener. As the board responds, it provides perspective, gives everyone a chance to be heard, and makes sure that all the topics have been well and fully addressed.

To summarize, the board should:

- *understand* the values of academic professionals and the culture of campus decision making;
- *know* something of wider trends in teaching and learning as well as the distinctive aspects of the institution's academic programs and policies;
- *actively monitor* programs and policies by questioning projects and proposals, as part of a chain of responsibility;
- *evaluate* programs and policies by ensuring that assessment is continuous and by exercising appropriate independent judgment;
- *ensure accountability* by creating the expectation that improvements will result from evaluations and by holding individuals and groups responsible for meeting goals; and

- *make decisions* on academic programs and policies by questioning, revising, returning, rejecting, and enacting proposals as appropriate.

These diverse aspects of its responsibility taken together move academic affairs high on the board's own agenda and provide an integrative focus for its work. This orientation also gives the board a constructive and significant role in academic affairs without challenging or undermining the normal patterns of academic decision making. It is consistent with the sense of ethical legitimacy and delegated academic authority embedded in the professional self-understanding of members of academic communities.

All participants in campus life know that academic decision making has its glories and its miseries. Its norms unleash powerful professional energies and achievements, but these same norms easily lose connection to the common good. When things are going well and resources are flowing, the problems in the system can be overlooked. As the need for change becomes insistent, however, flaws quickly show themselves.

It can become painfully clear, for example, that a single person or small group of faculty members can derail a promising program that otherwise appears to enjoy support. The primary issue is not opposition, nor even the negative behavior that may accompany it, but that those who choose to obstruct a new program do not have to answer for their actions. The authority to approve or disapprove of an academic program is not accompanied by personal responsibility for the decision. Given the challenges of modern organizational life and the constant need for change, surely this is one of the system's flaws.

The proposal for boards to ensure accountability in meeting goals addresses this structural weakness. The board's authority creates intensity around the issue and tightens the loose connection between authority and responsibility. As circumstances suggest, the board works closely with the president, the appropriate academic officers, and faculty members to stimulate suitable strategies to address unresolved problems or unfulfilled goals. The board's aim should be to summon others to the responsibility that properly belongs to them, not to undermine the work of the faculty or staff. To replace the weight of responsibility with bureaucratic rules or board interference is a mistake, for then the need to answer for decisions can be forevermore deflected or dodged. By challenging and pressing academic decision makers to fulfill their own commitments, the board taps a powerful professional obligation. The gap between academic authority and institutional responsibility can be narrowed and, at times, even closed.

The board's authority can be summarized by considering it in the context of its several functions—as authority over, with, and for others in

> **DATA POINT**
>
> **41%** of respondents said contributing to the mission of the institution was the most rewarding facet of serving on their board's academic affairs committee. **28%** said working with others on the committee. **22%** said learning about the academic programs.

the academic community.[2] The governing board is an institution's *final* authority, so it clearly has authority over the total institution. It can name and remove the president, and it decides every major issue of mission, size, program, or policy. Holding final authority is important, but the way a board uses that authority is more important. As the board energizes and balances a collaborative process of leadership, it affirms the basic responsibilities of others, monitors what they do, stands ready to use its authority to address problems, or corrects imbalances in reaching chosen objectives. In extremis, it may have to use its authority directly, even as authority against those who would harm the institution.

The board's authority *over* others is always a responsibility *with* others. In a modern, highly professional institution of higher learning in a democratic society, things could not be otherwise. All the information the board receives, as well as every proposal or recommendation, comes to it from others. For the board not to understand the dynamics of collaboration with academic professionals and with other university constituencies, for it to fail to appreciate both its limits and its possibilities in academic decisions, would be a serious error.

Finally, the board's authority is always *for* others. The board carries the heritage of the institution and responds to alumni. It represents the public interest, in quite direct ways if it is a state institution. It answers for the institution's commitment to its values, for its legal and financial integrity, for achievement of the institution's goals, and for the realization of its best possibilities. In a time when society harbors clashing expectations about higher education, the board's authority for the institution rises in significance. The board answers to the campus community as it strives to preserve, protect, and advance the best interests of students, staff, and faculty. To do so, it must understand and respect the traditions and beliefs of the place, even as it challenges the community to adapt to change. The board uses its authority to ensure that all the systems of academic authority and decision making within the institution are performing as they should. For this reason, were the board itself to violate the norms of good academic practice, should it take over the work of the faculty, it would create a profound crisis of confidence from which there would be no appeal.

We end where we began. The boards of trustees of academic institutions serve two masters. They are committed both to the cause of truth and to the effectiveness of the institution. They know that they have to integrate two competing systems of values within a single enterprise. On the one side is the danger of autonomy without responsibility, and on the other a narrowness that reduces education to commerce. Yet in knowing and telling the powerful story of the institution's identity, in summoning the community both to academic quality and institutional strength, trustees can make a decisive contribution to integrative, collaborative leadership.

As they press for greater accountability and more effective self-regulation among academic professionals, and for greater commitment from the faculty to the good of the institution that harbors them, trustees must remember the power of the academic calling to transcend self-interest and to serve students and society in response to a moral demand.

"In our cultural world," writes Burton R. Clark in *The Academic Life*, "the academy is still the place where devotion to knowledge remains most central, where it not merely survives but has great power. Many academic men and women know that power and still believe in it. They glow with that belief. In devotion to intellectual integrity, they find a demon who holds the fibers of their very lives." The academy needs leaders to sustain this vision. Trustees can be among them.

[1] Chait, Richard P., Thomas Holland, and Barbara E. Taylor. *The Effective Board of Trustees.* Phoenix: American Council on Education and Oryx Press, 1993.

[2] My friend and colleague, Professor Eric Mount of Centre College, introduced me to these distinctions.

Bibliography

American Association of University Professors. *1940 Statement of Principles and Interpretive Comments on Academic Freedom and Tenure*. Washington, D.C.: American Association of University Professors, 1984.

American Association of University Professors. *Statement on Government of Colleges and Universities*. Washington, D.C.: American Association of University Professors, 1984.

American Association of State Colleges and Universities. *Facing Change: Building the Faculty of the Future*. Washington, D.C.: American Association of State Colleges and Universities, 1999.

Association of Governing Boards of Universities and Colleges. "AGB Statement on Institutional Governance" and "Governing in the Public Trust: External Influences on Colleges and Universities." AGB Board Basics Series. Washington, D.C.: Association of Governing Boards of Universities and Colleges, 2001.

Astin, Alexander W. *Assessment for Excellence: The Philosophy and Practice of Assessment and Evaluation in Higher Education*. Phoenix: American Council on Education and Oryx Press, 1993.

Astin, Alexander W. *Four Critical Years: Effects of College on Beliefs, Attitudes, and Knowledge*. San Francisco: Jossey-Bass Publishers, 1977.

Astin, Alexander W. *What Matters in College? Four Critical Years Revisited*. San Francisco: Jossey-Bass Publishers, 1997.

Baldwin, Roger G., and Jay L. Chronister. *Teaching Without Tenure: Policies and Practices for a New Era*. Baltimore: Johns Hopkins University Press, 2001.

Barone, Carole, and Paul Hagner, eds. *Technology-Enhanced Teaching and Learning: Leading and Supporting the Transformation on Your Campus*. San Francisco: Jossey-Bass Publishers, 2001.

Benjamin, Ernst. "Part-Time Faculty, Full-Time Concerns." *Trusteeship*, Vol. 8, no. 4 (July/August 2000): 13-16.

Berberet, William G., and Linda McMillin. "The American Professoriate in Transition." *AGB Priorities*, No. 18 (Spring 2002).

Birnbaum, Robert. *How Academic Leadership Works: Understanding Success and Failure in the College Presidency*. San Francisco: Jossey-Bass Publishers, 1992.

Birnbaum, Robert. *How Colleges Work*. San Francisco: Jossey-Bass Publishers, 1988.

Bornstein, Rita. "Shared Governance and an Elusive Community." *Trusteeship*, Vol. 7, no. 2 (March/April 1999): 5.

Bowen, Howard R., and Jack H. Schuster. *American Professors: A National Resource Imperiled*. New York: Oxford University Press, 1986.

Bibliography

Boyer, Ernest L. *College: The Undergraduate Experience in America.* New York: Harper and Row, 1987.

Boyer, Ernest L. *Scholarship Reconsidered: Priorities of the Professoriate.* Princeton, N.J.: Carnegie Foundation for the Advancement of Teaching, 1990.

Breneman, David. "Voluntary Incentives to Forego Tenure." *New Pathways Working Paper Series.* Washington, D.C.: American Association for Higher Education, 1997.

Brown, John Seely. "Growing Up Digital: How the Web Changes Work, Education, and the Ways People Learn." *Change*, Vol. 32, no. 2 (March/April 2000): 11-20.

Chaffee, Ellen Earle, and William G. Tierney. *Collegiate Culture and Leadership Strategies.* New York: American Council on Education and Macmillan Publishing Company, 1988.

Chait, Richard P. "The Future of Academic Tenure." *AGB Priorities*, No. 3 (Spring 1995).

Chait, Richard P. and Associates. *Trustee Responsibility for Academic Affairs.* Washington, D.C.: Association of Governing Boards of Universities and Colleges, 1984.

Chait, Richard P., Thomas Holland, and Barbara E. Taylor. *The Effective Board of Trustees* Phoenix: American Council on Education and Oryx Press, 1993.

Chickering, Arthur W. and Linda Reisser. *Education and Identity.* 2nd ed. San Francisco: Jossey-Bass Publishers, 1993.

Clark, Burton R. *The Academic Life: Small Worlds, Different Worlds.* Princeton, N.J.: Carnegie Foundation for the Advancement of Teaching, 1987.

Brown, Christopher M., ed. *ASHE Reader on Organization and Governance in Higher Education.* 5th ed. Boston: Pearson Custom Publishing, 2000.

Cohen, Michael D. and James G. Marsh. *Leadership and Ambiguity: The American College President.* Boston: Harvard Business School Press, 1974.

The Commission on the Academic Presidency. *Renewing the Academic Presidency: Stronger Leadership for Tougher Times.* Washington, D.C.: Association of Governing Boards of Universities and Colleges, 1996.

Devlin, Maureen, Richard Larson, and Joel Meyerson, eds. *The Internet and the University.* Boulder: EDUCAUSE and The Forum for the Future of Higher Education, 2001.

Diamond, Robert M. *Aligning Faculty Rewards with Institutional Mission: Statements, Policies, and Guidelines.* Bolton, Mass.: Anker Publishing Company, Inc., 1999.

Dickeson, Robert C. *Prioritizing Academic Programs and Services: Reallocating Resources to Achieve Strategic Balance.* San Francisco: Jossey-Bass Publishers, 1999.

Ehrenberg, Ronald G. "Don't Shy Away From Retirement Questions." *Trusteeship*, Vol. 9, no. 4 (July/August 2001): 8-13.

Euben, Donna R. "The Faculty Handbook as a Contract: Is It Enforceable?" *Academe*, Vol. 84, no. 5 (September/October 1998): 87.

Ferren, Ann S., and Rick Slavings. *Investing in Quality: Tools for Improving Curricular Efficiency.* Washington, D.C.: Association of American Colleges and Universities, 2000.

Finkin, Matthew, ed. *The Case for Tenure*. Ithaca, N.Y.: Cornell University Press, 1996.

Fisher, James L. *The Board and the President*. New York: American Council on Education and Macmillan Publishing Company, 1991.

Fisher, James L. and James V. Koch. *Presidential Leadership: Making a Difference*. Phoenix: Oryx Press, 1996.

Gaff, Jerry G., and James L. Ratcliff, eds. *Handbook of the Undergraduate Curriculum: A Comprehensive Guide to Purposes, Structures, Practices, and Change*. San Francisco: Jossey-Bass Publishers, 1997.

Gappa, Judith M. and David W. Leslie. "Two Faculties or One? The Conundrum of Part-Timers in a Bifurcated Workforce." *New Pathways Working Paper Series*. Washington, D.C.: American Association for Higher Education, 1997.

Gappa, Judith M., and Shelley M. MacDermid. "Work, Family, and the Faculty Career." *New Pathways Working Paper Series*. Washington, D.C.: American Association for Higher Education, 1997.

Gardner, Howard. *Leading Minds: An Anatomy of Leadership*. New York: Basic Books, 1995.

Gardner, John W. *On Leadership*. New York: Free Press, 1993.

Gayle, Dennis J., et al. "Turning Culture Clash Into Collaboration." *Trusteeship* Vol. 7, no. 3 (May/June 1999): 24-27.

"Greater Expectations: The Commitment to Quality as a Nation Goes to College." *Liberal Education,* Vol. 85, no. 2 (Spring 1999): 19-23.

Gumport, Patricia J. "Divided We Govern?" *AAC&U Peer Review*, Vol. 3, no. 3 (Spring 2001): 14-17.

Hamilton, Neil. "The Search for Common Ground on Academic Governance," *AAC&U Peer Review*, Vol. 3, no. 3 (Spring 2001): 12-13.

Heifetz, Ronald A. *Leadership Without Easy Answers*. Cambridge: Harvard University Press, 1994.

Ingram, Richard T., and Associates. *Governing Independent Colleges and Universities: A Handbook for Trustees, Chief Executives, and Other Campus Leaders*. San Francisco: Jossey-Bass Publishers, 1993.

Kerr, Clark, and Marian Gade. *The Guardians: Boards of Trustees of American Colleges and Universities*. Washington, D.C.: Association of Governing Boards of Universities and Colleges, 1989.

Kouzes, James M., and Barry K. Posner. *The Leadership Challenge: How To Get Extraordinary Things Done in Organizations*. San Francisco: Jossey-Bass Publishers, 1996.

Kouzes, James M., and Barry K. Posner. *The Leadership Challenge*. 3rd ed. San Francisco: Jossey-Bass Publishers, 2002.

Kuh, George D. "Assessing What Really Matters in Student Learning: Inside the National Survey of Student Engagement." *Change*, Vol. 33, no. 3 (May/June 2001): 10-17, 66.

Kuh, George D., John J. Schuh, and Elizabeth J. Whitt. *Involving Colleges: Successful Approaches to Fostering Student Learning and Development Outside the Classroom*. San Francisco: Jossey-Bass Publishers, 1991.

Leap, Terry L. *Tenure, Discrimination, and the Courts*. 2nd edition. Ithaca, N.Y.: ILR Press and Cornell University Press, 1995.

Bibliography

Licata, Christine M. "Precepts for Post-Tenure Reviews." *Trusteeship*, Vol. 7, no. 6 (November/December 1999): 8-13.

Licata, Christine M., and Joseph C. Morreale. "Post-Tenure Review: Policies, Practices, Precautions." *New Pathways Working Paper Series*. Washington, D.C.: American Association for Higher Education, 1997.

Madsen, Holly. "Case Studies: Life Without Tenure." In *AGB Priorities*, No. 3 (Spring 1995): 10.

Magner, Denise K. "Battle Over Academic Control Pits Faculty Against Governing Board at George Mason U." *Chronicle of Higher Education* (June, 18, 1999): A14.

Magner, Denise K. "Faculty Accuses George Mason U. Board of Improper Meddling With Curriculum," *Chronicle of Higher Education* (June 2, 2000): A20.

Massy, William F., and Joel W. Meyerson, eds. *Revitalizing Higher Education: Stanford Forum for Higher Education Futures*. Princeton: Peterson's Guides, 1995.

Merisotis, Jamie P., and Ronald A. Phipps. "What's the Difference? Outcomes of Distance vs. Traditional Classroom-Based Learning." *Change*, Vol. 31, no. 3 (May/June 1999): 12-17.

McMillin, Linda, and William G. Berberet, eds. *A New Academic Compact: Revisioning the Relationship Between Faculty and Their Institutions*. Bolton, Mass.: Anker Publishing Co., Inc., 2002.

Morrill, Richard L. "Academic Planning: Values and Decision Making." In *Ethics and Higher Education*. William M. May, ed. New York: American Council on Education and Macmillan Publishing Company, 1990: 69-83.

Morrill, Richard L. and Edward D. Eddy, "Living with Tenure Without Quotas." *Liberal Education*, Vol. 61, no. 3 (October 1975): 399-417.

Palomba, Catherine A. and Trudy W. Banta. *Assessment Essentials: Planning, Implementing, and Improving Assessment in Higher Education*. San Francisco: Jossey-Bass Publishers, 1999.

The Project on Faculty Appointments at the Harvard Graduate School of Education. *FAPA: Faculty Appointment Policy Archive*. Cambridge, Mass.: Harvard Education Publishing Group, 2001. [CD-ROM]

Perley, James E. "Faculty and Governing Boards: Building Bridges." *Academe*, Vol. 83, no. 5 (September/October 1997): 34-37.

Reed, William S. *Financial Responsibilities of Governing Boards*. Washington, D.C.: Association of Governing Boards of Universities and Colleges and the National Association of College and University Business Officers, 2001.

Rice, R. Eugene . "Making a Place for the New American Scholar." *New Pathways Working Paper Series*. Washington, D.C.: American Association for Higher Education, 1996.

Rice, R. Eugene, Mary Deane Sorcinelli, and Ann E. Austin. "Heeding New Voices: Academic Careers for a New Generation." *New Pathways Working Paper Series*. Washington, D.C.: American Association for Higher Education, 2000.

Rodas, Daniel J., et al. "Applying Contribution Margin Analysis in a Research University." *In Revitalizing Higher Education: Stanford Forum for Higher Education*. William F. Massy and Joel W. Meyerson, eds. Princeton: Peterson's Guides, 1995. 73-87.

Rudolph, Frederick. *Curriculum: A History of the American Undergraduate Course of Study Since 1636.* San Francisco: Jossey-Bass Publishers, 1993. Reprint.

Schmidt, Peter. "SUNY Faculty Groups Lack Faith in Board," *Chronicle of Higher Education,* Vol. 46, no. 13 (May 14, 1999): A40.

Schneider, Carol Geary, and Robert Shoenberg. *Contemporary Understandings of Liberal Education.* Washington, D.C.: Association of American Colleges and Universities, 1998.

Shechner, Mark. "Ozymandias on the Erie: What Is It Like to Teach in a State Where Politicians No Longer Care About Public Higher Education?" *Academe,* Vol. 86, no. 6 (November/December 2000): 24-33.

Taylor, Barbara E., et al. *Strategic Analysis: Using Comparative Data to Understand Your Institution.* Washington, D.C.: Association of Governing Boards of Universities and Colleges, 1991.

Tierney, William G., ed. *The Responsive University: Restructuring for High Performance.* Baltimore: The Johns Hopkins University Press, 1998.

Trower, Cathy A. "Employment Practices in the Professions: Fresh Ideas from Inside and Outside the Academy." *New Pathways Working Paper Series.* Washington, D.C.: American Association for Higher Education, 1998.

Trower, Cathy A., ed. *Policies on Faculty Appointment: Standard Practices and Unusual Arrangements.* Bolton, Mass.: Anker Publishing Company, Inc., 2000.

Weigel, Van B.0. "E-Learning and the Tradeoff Between Richness and Reach in Higher Education." *Change,* Vol. 33, no. 5 (September/October 2000): 10-15.

Weingartner, Rudolph H. *Undergraduate Education: Goals and Means.* Phoenix: American Council on Education and Oryx Press, 1993.

Wood, Richard J. "Academic Affairs Committee." AGB *Board Basics Series.* Washington, D.C.: Association of Governing Boards of Universities and Colleges, 1997.

Zahorski, Kenneth J., and Roger Cognard. *Reconsidering Faculty Roles and Rewards: Promising Practices for Institutional Transformation and Enhanced Learning.* Washington, D.C.: Council for Independent Colleges, 1999.

AGB's Zwingle Resource Center provides members with an extensive annotated bibliography of related readings online at www.agb.org. For additional information about this or other trusteeship, governance or higher education issues, visit the web site, contact AGB's Zwingle Resource Center at 202-296-8400, or e-mail your questions to zrc@agb.org.

All AGB publications are available at www.agb.org.

About the Author

Following ten years as president of the University of Richmond, Richard L. Morrill in July 1998 became chancellor and distinguished university professor of ethics and democratic values. He previously was president of Centre College in Kentucky from 1982-88 and president of Salem College in North Carolina from 1979-82.

Morrill began his teaching career in 1967 at Wells College in New York before moving to Chatham College in Pennsylvania, where he served as associate professor of religion, executive assistant to the president, and associate provost. He was chief of staff to the provost of Pennsylvania State University from 1977-79.

Morrill received his A.B. in history from Brown University in 1961, graduating magna cum laude; his B.D. in religious thought in 1964 from Yale University, where he was a Woodrow Wilson Fellow and the recipient of the Tew Prize for excellence in studies; and his Ph.D. in religion from the Duke University Graduate School of Arts and Sciences, where he was a James B. Duke Fellow. He studied in France as an undergraduate, principally at L'Institut D'Études Politiques.

Recipient of honorary degrees from four institutions, including the École des Haute Études Internationales in Paris, Morrill is a member of the Order of Academic Palms. In 1997, he served as a member of the Organization for Economic Development's four-person team to evaluate the initial years of study in French universities.

Morrill has written widely on issues of values and ethics in higher education and has published several articles and made numerous presentations on strategic planning and leadership for colleges and universities. He served on the board of the Association of American Colleges and Universities and as president of the Southern Association of Colleges and Schools. He currently is a board member of three corporations and of several nonprofit organizations, including the Teagle Foundation, the Christian Children's Fund, and the Library of Virginia Foundation.

Appendix I

Results of an AGB Survey on the Board's Responsibility for Academic Programs

In 2000, AGB began a project on the board's responsibilities for academic programs. It included a national survey of board members and academic leaders to identify current practices, attitudes, and academic and faculty issues affecting the work of boards and board committees. The data that appear in this appendix come from this survey, which was conducted in spring 2001. This information provides detail on the "Data Points" located throughout the book. The survey results are presented in full in an Occasional Paper available through AGB.

The Survey

The survey was based on a similar 1984 survey conducted for the AGB book *Trustee Responsibility for Academic Affairs*, by Richard Chait and Associates. For *Strategic Leadership in Academic Affairs*, the 1984 survey was updated to reflect changes that have taken place in higher education in the ensuing years. For example, the current survey asks questions related to technology, distance learning, and intellectual property rights. By using the original survey and comparing data from the two surveys, it was possible to identify changes in common practices of boards in the area of academic affairs, as well as trends in the academic issues.

The survey gathered six types of information:
- The importance respondents attached to academic and faculty issues commonly addressed by colleges and universities.
- The actual practices of boards—the issues brought to them and the degree to which they were engaged in decision making about those issues.
- Critical academic issues facing institutions, both now and in the near future.
- Attitudes toward the board's responsibility for academic affairs.
- Sources and quality of information boards receive on academic matters.
- Demographic information about academic affairs committees of boards.

For the first three categories, comparative information was available from the 1984 survey.

The Process and Participants

In April 2001, surveys were sent to 364 chief academic officers and 176 board members from public and private institutions, all members of AGB. Board members were those chairing academic affairs committees or, in the absence of such a committee, a trustee with special interest in the area. Chief academic officers were the highest ranking academic officers on their campuses, whether academic vice president, dean, or provost. Survey recipients were self-selected, having previously indicated interest in participating.

Appendix I

Of the 540 who received the survey, 308 completed it.

Approximately one-third of participants were board members, and two-thirds were chief academic officers. Approximately one-quarter were from public institutions, three-quarters from private. The table below identifies the numbers of participants by position and institutional type—public or private.

Number of Survey Participants by Position and Institutional Type

Institution	CAO	Board	Total
Public	50	16	66
Private	154	88	242
All	204	104	308

Participants also were identified by their institution's Carnegie classification. (2000 version). The most frequently represented categories were the master's colleges and universities and the baccalaureate colleges, each constituting about one-third of the respondents. The doctoral/research universities constituted about one-tenth, as did the specialized institutions (seminaries, medical schools, and law schools, for example). Associate's colleges made up about 5 percent, and another 5 percent chose not to identify themselves by classification.

The Responses

Data from the survey responses have been summarized and presented as "Data Points" to support or amplify the information in this book. What follows is additional detail on those responses, arranged in the order in which the Data Points appear in the book. For greater detail and discussion, see AGB Occasional Paper No. 50, "A National Survey on Boards' Involvement in Academic Affairs," by Susan Whealler Johnston, director of AGB's independent-sector programs and director of AGB's project on boards and academic affairs.

All responses are presented as percentages, which because of rounding may not total 100. In a few cases, percentages do not total 100 because respondents gave more than one answer.

Chapter 1, Data Point 1 (page 6)

What is your level of agreement with this statement: Boards and faculty need a shared understanding of their different responsibilities for governance of academic programs.

	STRONGLY AGREE	AGREE	NO OPINION	DISAGREE	STRONGLY DISAGREE
Public	53.8%	46.2%	0.0%	0.0%	0.0%
Private	67.4	30.2	1.2	0.0	1.2
All	65.7	32.3	1.0	0.0	1.0

Chapter 2, Data Point 1 (page 12)

For your institution, how important is establishing a plan for assessing student-learning outcomes?

	DON'T KNOW	NOT IMPORTANT	MODERATELY IMPORTANT	VERY IMPORTANT
Public	0.0	8.9	26.7	64.4
Private	2.2	14.7	39.9	43.2
All	1.7	13.6	37.3	47.4

Chapter 2, Data Point 2 (page 15)

What three academic issues are currently most important to your institution?
What three issues will be most important in the next three to five years?

PRIVATE IN 2001

1.	Assessment	44.5
2.	Faculty hiring/salaries/work load	38.4
3.	Faculty assessment/development	38.0
4.	Student enrollment	36.2
5.	Program development	32.3
6.	Technology/distance learning	25.8

IN 3-5 YEARS

1.	Faculty hiring/salaries/work load	46.5
2.	Technology and distance learning	42.9
3.	Assessment	35.4
4.	Faculty development	27.4
5.	Student enrollment	26.5
6.	Program development	23.0

PUBLIC IN 2001

1.	Student enrollment	54.4
2.	Assessment	43.9
3.	Faculty hiring/salaries	36.8
4.	Faculty development	31.6
5.	Program development	28.1
6.	Technology/distance learning	24.6

IN 3-5 YEARS

1.	Faculty hiring/salaries	47.4
2.	Student enrollment	40.4
3.	Budget	38.6
4.	Assessment	33.3
5/6.	Technology/distance learning	26.3
5/6.	Program development	26.3

Chapter 2, Data Point 2 continued on page 110

Appendix I

Chapter 2, Data Point 2 continued from page 109

ALL IN 2001		
1.	Assessment	44.4
2.	Student enrollment	39.9
3.	Faculty hiring/salaries	38.1
4.	Faculty development	36.7
5.	Program development	31.5
6.	Technology/distance learning	25.5

IN 3-5 YEARS		
1.	Faculty hiring/salaries	46.5
2.	Technology/distance learning	39.4
3.	Assessment	34.9
4.	Student enrollment	29.2
5/6.	Faculty development	25.0
5/6.	Budget	25.0

Note: Because respondents gave multiple answers, percentages do not total 100.

Chapter 3, Data Point 1 (page 22)

In the past five years, has your board discussed establishing new academic programs?

	2001		**1984**	
	Yes	**No**	**Yes**	**No**
Public	77.8	22.2	71.0	29.0
Private	58.5	41.5	70.8	29.2
All	62.8	37.2	70.9	29.1

Chapter 3, Data Point 2 (page 26)

For your institution, how important is revising general education to reflect shifts in thinking about students' educational needs?

2001				
	DON'T KNOW	**NOT IMPORTANT**	**MODERATELY IMPORTANT**	**VERY IMPORTANT**
Public	2.2	11.1	46.7	40.0
Private	2.2	12.1	48.9	36.8
All	2.2	11.9	48.5	37.4

1984				
	DON'T KNOW	**NOT IMPORTANT**	**MODERATELY IMPORTANT**	**VERY IMPORTANT**
Public	3.9	27.0	46.0	23.1
Private	5.5	29.5	40.1	24.9
All	4.6	28.1	43.3	23.9

Chapter 3, Data Point 3 (page 29)

For your institution, how important is developing new academic programs in response to changing internal demand?

	DON'T KNOW	NOT IMPORTANT	MODERATELY IMPORTANT	VERY IMPORTANT
Public	0.0	8.9	24.4	66.7
Private	0.5	8.1	40.0	51.4
All	0.4	8.3	37.0	54.3

Chapter 3, Data Point 4 (page 33)

For your institution, how important is modifying policies on faculty work load to promote research and publication?

	DON'T KNOW	NOT IMPORTANT	MODERATELY IMPORTANT	VERY IMPORTANT
Public	8.9	40.0	40.0	11.1
Private	2.7	56.3	31.1	9.8
All	3.9	53.1	32.9	10.1

CARNEGIE CLASSIFICATION	DON'T KNOW	NOT IMPORTANT	MODERATELY IMPORTANT	VERY IMPORTANT
Doctoral	3.8	30.8	61.5	3.8
Master's	5.9	54.1	28.2	11.8
Baccalaureate	1.3	53.2	32.5	13.0

Chapter 3, Data Point 5 (page 35)

For your institution, how important is changing admissions standards to alter the size, composition, or quality of the student body?

2001				
	DON'T KNOW	NOT IMPORTANT	MODERATELY IMPORTANT	VERY IMPORTANT
Public	4.4	6.7	48.9	40.0
Private	7.1	39.3	36.1	17.5
All	6.6	32.9	38.6	21.9

1984				
	DON'T KNOW	NOT IMPORTANT	MODERATELY IMPORTANT	VERY IMPORTANT
Public	8.4	52.7	25.4	13.5
Private	9.5	49.6	32.4	8.5
All	8.9	51.3	28.6	11.3

Appendix I

Chapter 3, Data Point 6 (page 36)

What three academic issues are currently most important to your institution?
What three issues will be most important in the next 3 to 5 years?

PRIVATE IN 2001

1.	Assessment	44.5
2.	Faculty hiring/salaries/work load	38.4
3.	Faculty assessment/development	38.0
4.	Student enrollment	36.2
5.	Program development	32.3
6.	Technology/distance learning	25.8

IN 3-5 YEARS

1.	Faculty hiring/salaries/work load	46.5
2.	Technology/distance learning	42.9
3.	Assessment	35.4
4.	Faculty development	27.4
5.	Student enrollment	26.5
6.	Program development	23.0

PUBLIC IN 2001

1.	Student enrollment	54.4
2.	Assessment	43.9
3.	Faculty hiring/salaries	36.8
4.	Faculty development	31.6
5.	Program development	28.1
6.	Technology/distance learning	24.6

IN 3-5 YEARS

1.	Faculty hiring/salaries	47.4
2.	Student enrollment	40.4
3.	Budget	38.6
4.	Assessment	33.3
5/6.	Technology/distance learning	26.3
5/6.	Program development	26.3

ALL IN 2001

1.	Assessment	44.4
2.	Student enrollment	39.9
3.	Faculty hiring/salaries	38.1
4.	Faculty development	36.7
5.	Program development	31.5
6.	Technology/distance learning	25.5

IN 3-5 YEARS

1.	Faculty hiring/salaries	46.5
2.	Technology/distance learning	39.4
3.	Assessment	34.9
4.	Student enrollment	29.2
5/6.	Faculty development	25.0
5/6.	Budget	25.0

Chapter 3, Data Point 7 (page 40)

For your institution, how important is reviewing the strengths and weaknesses of existing academic programs?

2001

	DON'T KNOW	NOT IMPORTANT	MODERATELY IMPORTANT	VERY IMPORTANT
Public	0.0	0.0	20.0	80.0
Private	0.5	2.2	20.0	77.3
All	0.4	1.7	20.0	77.8

1984

	DON'T KNOW	NOT IMPORTANT	MODERATELY IMPORTANT	VERY IMPORTANT
Public	0.3	4.4	31.3	64.0
Private	0.4	6.6	34.0	56.0
All	0.4	5.4	32.5	61.7

Chapter 4, Data Point 1 (page 44)

For your institution, how important is establishing a planning and budgeting process that leads to prioritized allocation of resources to academic areas?

2001

	DON'T KNOW	NOT IMPORTANT	MODERATELY IMPORTANT	VERY IMPORTANT
Public	2.3	6.8	18.2	72.7
Private	1.1	13.3	35.6	50.0
All	1.3	12.1	32.1	54.5

1984

	DON'T KNOW	NOT IMPORTANT	MODERATELY IMPORTANT	VERY IMPORTANT
Public	1.0	11.1	28.7	59.1
Private	1.2	15.9	26.0	56.8
All	1.1	13.3	27.5	58.1

Appendix I

Chapter 4, Data Point 2 (page 49)

What is your board's role in decision making related to faculty compensation policies?

	Public	Private	All
The board makes the decision about this issue, though it might seek the opinions of others before doing so.	27.3	19.7	21.5
The board directs the administration to take action on this issue after consultation.	50.0	49.7	49.7
The board receives information about the issue, but takes no action on it.	9.1	22.4	19.4
This issue would not come to the board at all.	13.6	8.2	9.4
Don't know	0.0	0.0	0.0

Chapter 5, Data Point 1 (page 54)

What is your board's role in decision making related to approving the general education curriculum?

	Public	Private	All
The board makes the decision about this issue, though it might seek the opinions of others before doing so.	9.3	6.8	7.4
The board directs the administration to take action on this issue after consultation.	30.2	26.0	27.0
The board receives information about the issue, but takes no action on it.	32.6	43.2	40.7
This issue would not come to the board at all.	27.9	21.9	23.3
Don't know	0.0	2.1	1.6

Chapter 5, Data Point 2 (page 60)

What is your level of agreement with this statement: In certain circumstances, it is appropriate for a board to override faculty in matters of curriculum?

	STRONGLY AGREE	AGREE	NO OPINION	DISAGREE	STRONGLY DISAGREE
All	3.0	54.5	8.1	24.2	10.1

Chapter 6, Data Point 1 (page 63)

In the past five years, has your board discussed establishing a policy on faculty work load?

	YES	NO
Public	37.0	63.0
Private	18.1	81.9
All	29.8	70.2

Chapter 6, Data Point 2 (page 65)

For your institution, how important are questions of academic freedom in discussions of teaching, curriculum, and faculty activity?

	DON'T KNOW	NOT IMPORTANT	MODERATELY IMPORTANT	VERY IMPORTANT
Public	2.2	35.6	42.2	20.0
Private	3.9	46.4	35.9	13.8
All	3.6	44.2	37.2	15.0

Chapter 6, Data Point 3 (page 66)

What is your board's role in decision making related to tenure and promotion policies?

	Public	Private	All
The board makes the decision about this issue, though it might seek the opinions of others before doing so.	18.2	12.8	14.1
The board directs the administration to take action on this issue after consultation.	38.6	40.5	40.1
The board receives information about the issue, but takes no action on it.	22.7	31.1	29.2
This issue would not come to the board at all.	20.5	13.5	15.1
Don't know	0.0	2.0	1.6

Chapter 6, Data Point 4 (page 68)

For your institution, how important is changing faculty appointment, promotion, tenure, and retirement policies to achieve greater staffing flexibility?

	DON'T KNOW	NOT IMPORTANT	MODERATELY IMPORTANT	VERY IMPORTANT
Public	0.0	28.9	46.7	24.4
Private	1.6	34.6	41.8	22.0
All	1.3	33.5	42.7	22.5

Appendix I

Chapter 6, Data Point 5 (page 70)

For your institution, how important is establishing a plan for post-tenure review?

	DON'T KNOW	NOT IMPORTANT	MODERATELY IMPORTANT	VERY IMPORTANT
Public	4.5	26.7	44.4	24.4
Private	5.1	32.4	33.5	29.0
All	5.0	31.2	35.7	28.1

Chapter 6, Data Point 6 (page 72)

In the past five years, has your board discussed establishing an early retirement policy for faculty?

	YES	NO
Public	48.1	51.9
Private	39.4	60.6
All	41.3	58.7

Chapter 6, Data Point 7 (page 74)

For your institution, how important is establishing alternatives to tenure?

	DON'T KNOW	NOT IMPORTANT	MODERATELY IMPORTANT	VERY IMPORTANT
Public	1.7	53.3	28.3	16.7
Private	3.0	49.6	30.2	17.2
All	2.7	50.2	30.0	17.1

Chapter 6, Data Point 8 (page 79)

For your institution, how important is establishing faculty development programs to enhance the use of technology in teaching?

	DON'T KNOW	NOT IMPORTANT	MODERATELY IMPORTANT	VERY IMPORTANT
Public	1.7	15.0	33.3	50.0
Private	2.6	15.5	36.2	45.7
All	2.4	15.7	35.5	46.4

Chapter 6, Data Point 8 (page 79)

For your institution, how important is establishing faculty development programs to support professional development needs at different stages of the faculty career?

	DON'T KNOW	NOT IMPORTANT	MODERATELY IMPORTANT	VERY IMPORTANT
Public	0.0	4.4	51.1	44.5
Private	1.6	16.5	46.7	35.2
All	1.3	14.1	47.6	37.0

Chapter 6, Data Point 8 (page 79)

For your institution, how important is establishing faculty development programs to enhance faculty satisfaction?

	DON'T KNOW	NOT IMPORTANT	MODERATELY IMPORTANT	VERY IMPORTANT
Public	0.0	6.7	64.4	28.9
Private	1.7	17.8	53.3	27.2
All	1.3	15.5	55.6	27.6

Chapter 6, Data Point 9 (page 80)

For your institution, how important is establishing a plan for hiring more women and minority faculty members?

2001

	DON'T KNOW	NOT IMPORTANT	MODERATELY IMPORTANT	VERY IMPORTANT
Public	0.0	3.4	43.1	53.4
Private	3.8	15.8	47.9	32.5
All	3.1	13.3	46.8	36.9

1984

	DON'T KNOW	NOT IMPORTANT	MODERATELY IMPORTANT	VERY IMPORTANT
Public	2.8	27.5	41.3	28.3
Private	3.2	45.8	35.3	15.6
All	3.0	35.9	38.6	22.5

Chapter 7, Data Point 1 (page 83)

What areas are assigned to your board's academic affairs committee?

	All	Public	Private
Academic and faculty issues	49.7	34.1	54.2
Academic and faculty issues, enrollment management, and student services	20.2	39.0	14.8
Academic and faculty issues, and enrollment management	18.8	17.1	19.0
Academic and faculty issues, and student services	9.3	7.3	9.9
All others	3.3	9.8	1.4
Not applicable	1.6	2.4	1.4
Technology	1.1	0.0	1.4

Appendix I

Chapter 7, Data Point 2 (page 86)

What is your level of agreement with this statement: It is important for boards to have a significant voice in the nature and shape of academic programs offered by an institution.

	STRONGLY AGREE	AGREE	NO OPINION	DISAGREE	STRONGLY DISAGREE
Public	38.5	30.8	7.7	23.1	0.0
Private	16.3	60.5	3.5	18.6	1.2
All	19.2	56.6	4.0	19.2	1.0

Chapter 7, Data Point 3 (page 87)

For your institution, how important is developing new academic programs in response to the interests of business and industry?

	DON'T KNOW	NOT IMPORTANT	MODERATELY IMPORTANT	VERY IMPORTANT
Public	0.0	4.4	37.8	57.8
Private	1.1	21.7	45.7	31.5
All	0.9	18.3	44.1	36.7

Chapter 7, Data Point 4 (page 90)

What is your level of agreement with this statement: It is important for a board's academic affairs committee to have one or more voting members who have academic backgrounds (such as presidents, deans, or faculty from other institutions).

	STRONGLY AGREE	AGREE	NO OPINION	DISAGREE	STRONGLY DISAGREE
Public	15.4	15.4	15.4	38.5	15.4
Private	52.3	33.7	4.7	8.1	1.2
All	47.5	31.3	6.1	12.1	3.0

Conclusion, Data Point 1 (page 95)

What do you find most enjoyable or personally rewarding about serving on your board's academic affairs committee?

Top Responses	All	Public	Private
Contributing to the mission	41.1	53.8	39.0
Relationships with committee members	27.8	7.7	31.2
Learning about educational programs and policies	22.2	15.4	23.4
Making a difference in the institution	21.1	30.8	19.5
Having a shared purpose with other committee members	15.6	15.4	15.6
Contributing to successful outcomes	13.3	30.8	10.4

Note: Because respondents gave multiple answers, percentages do not total 100.

Appendix II

Advisory Group to the Academic Affairs Project

Paula Brownlee
President Emerita, Association of American
Colleges and Universities
Washington, D.C.

Joel Cunningham
Vice Chancellor and President,
University of the South
Sewanee, Tenn.

Robert C. Dickeson
Senior Vice President for Higher
Education Policy, Research, and Evaluation
Lumina Foundation for Education
Indianapolis

Judith Eaton
President, Council for Higher Education
Accreditation
Washington, D.C.

Richard Ekman
President, Council of Independent Colleges
Washington, D.C.

Bobby Fong
President, Butler University
Indianapolis

Susan D. Gotsch
Vice President for Academic Affairs
Hartwick College
Oneonta, N.Y.

Brian L. Hawkins
President, EDUCAUSE
Washington, D.C.

Margaret Healy
President Emerita, Rosemont College
Rosemont, Pa.

Barbara Hetrick
Vice President for Academic Affairs
College of Wooster
Wooster, Ohio

David E. Maxwell
President, Drake University
Des Moines, Iowa

Linda McMillin
Chair, Department of History
Susquehanna University
Selinsgrove, Pa.

Terrence J. MacTaggart
Distinguished Faculty, University of Maine;
Senior Fellow, AGB
Washington, D.C.

R. Eugene Rice
Director, Forum on Faculty Roles and
Rewards, American Association for
Higher Education
Washington, D.C.

Thomas E. Scheye
Distinguished Service Faculty
Loyola College in Maryland
Baltimore

Susan Whealler Johnston
Project Director, Director of Independent
Sector Programs, AGB
Washington, D.C.

E. B. Wilson
Chairman Emeritus,
Board of Trustees, St. Lawrence University
Canton, N.Y.

Index

A

AAUP. *See* American Association of University Professors

ABA. *See* American Bar Association

Academic affairs committee
faculty personnel policies and decisions, 88–89
function of, 83–87
importance of, 83
membership, 89–91
program approval, 87–88

Academic budgets
benchmarking information, 46
budget committees, 44–45
consortia, 46
containing costs, 48–50
financial aid, 47–48
financial models, 45–46
information systems, 45–46
planning, 44–45
responsibility center budgeting, 46–47
strategic analysis, 43–50
tuition revenues, 47–48

Academic decision making, 1

The Academic Life, 97

Academic majors, 25–27

Academic professionals
academic affairs committee, 83–92
administrative review, 77
alternatives to tenure system, 73–74
autonomy of, 3–4
"best practices," 75
commitment to knowledge, 4–5
contract system, 73–74
early retirement incentives, 71–72
ethical misconduct, 67
faculty development, 78–79
financial exigency and, 67
first faculty position appointment, 62
grievance procedures, 77
levels of recommendation, 76
mandatory retirement elimination, 65
mid-service review, 76
monitoring policies and procedures, 80–81
nature of appointments, 75
non-tenure-track positions, 69
part-time faculty, 69–70
peer review, 76
performance feedback, 75
portfolios, 76
post-tenure review, 70–71
professional incompetence, 67
program discontinuance, 67
promotion, 78
provisional period, 75
responsibilities of, 62–63
role of, 13–14
salaries and benefits, 48–50
statistical profiles, 79–80
temporary appointments, 69
tenure decisions, 5
tenure files, 76
tenure quotas, 68–69
tenure system, 63–78
values formation, 61–62

Academic programs
academic majors, 25–27
accreditation, 40–42
assessing quality, 36–40
concentrations, 28
distribution requirements, 23
enrollment planning and management, 34–36
general education, 22–25
graduate programs, 30–31
interdisciplinary studies, 28–30
minors, 28
monitoring general education programs, 25
professional studies, 27–28
program review, 40
research, 31–33
student development, 33–34
trustees' role, 21–22, 25

Accreditation, 27, 40–42

Adequate cause terminations, 67–68

Age Discrimination in Employment Act, 65

American Association of University Professors, 63, 66

American Bar Association, 41

Association of American Colleges and Universities, 14

Autonomy
academic professionals and, 3–4
finding shared values, 5–6

B

Budgets. *See* Academic budgets

C

Campus Compact, 33–34

Campus life, 33–34
Campus Outreach Opportunity League, 33–34
Change and *Liberal Education* magazines, 90
Chief academic officer, 84
Chronicle of Higher Education, 91
COFHE. See Consortium on Financing Higher Education
Collaborative learning, 13
Colleges. See Higher education
Competencies, 14
Computer technology, 15–16
Concentrations, academic, 28
Consortium on Financing Higher Education, 46
COOL. See Campus Outreach Opportunity League
Curriculum content, 54–55, 93–94

D

Decision making. See also Academic programs; Tenure system
  academic, 1–2
  leadership and, 6–8
  organizational, 1
  shared values, 5–6
  strategic, 6–8
  tensions in relations, 2–3, 5
  trustees' contributions, 7–8, 53–60
Defined-benefit retirement plans, 72
Distance learning, 15–16
Distribution requirements, 23
Doctoral programs, 30–31

E

Educational trends. See Higher education
Educators. See Academic professionals
The Effective Board of Trustees, 93–94
Engaged learning, 14–15
Enrollment planning, 34–36
Ethical misconduct, 67
Exchange agreements, 17
Experiential learning, 13

F

Fact Books, 38
Faculty development programs, 78–79
Faculty members. See Academic professionals
Fellowships, 30–31
Financial aid, 47–48
Financial exigency, 67
Financial models, 45–46

G

General education programs, 22–25, 55–57
Governing boards. See Trustees
Graduate programs, 30–31, 32
Grants, 32
Grievance procedures
  tenure system and, 77

H

HEDS. *See* Higher Education Data Service
High-stakes tests, 36
Higher education. *See also* Academic professionals; Academic programs
  academic affairs committee, 83–91
  academic budgets, 32, 43–50
  access to, 11–12
  assessing student-learning outcomes, 12
  attrition, 12
  completion rates, 12
  engaged learning, 14–15
  information technology, 15–16
  internationalization, 16–19
  learning movement, 12–14
  multicultural studies, 16–19
  role of educators, 13–14
  trustee responsibilities, 51–60
Higher Education Data Service, 46

I

Incompetence, 67
Information technology, 15–16
Institutional accreditation, 40–42
Interdisciplinary studies, 28–30
International students, 17
Internationalization, 16–19
Internet, 15–16
Internships, 13
Island programs, 17

K

Knowledge, commitment to, 4–5

L

Leadership
  decision making and, 6–8
Learning communities, 13
Learning movement, 12–14
Liberal arts colleges
  general education case study, 55–58

M

Majors, academic, 25–27
Mandatory retirement
  tenure system and, 65

Masters programs, 30–31
Minors, academic, 28
Multicultural studies, 16–19

N

National Collegiate Athletic Association, 54
National Survey of Student Engagement, 12, 14
NCAA. *See* National Collegiate Athletic Association

O

Organizational decision making, 1
Overhead, 32

P

Part-time faculty, 69–70
Peer interaction, 13
Peer review, 76
Post-tenure review, 70–71
Professional incompetence, 67
Professional studies, 27–28
Professors. *See* Academic professionals
Program discontinuance
  academic professionals and, 67
Program review, 40
Promotions, 78
Provisional periods, 75
Provost, 84

Q

Quality assessment, 36–40
Quota systems, 68–69

R

Regional accreditation, 40–42
Research
  grant overhead, 32
  sponsored, 32
  strategic role of, 31–33
  student projects, 13
  unsponsored, 32–33
Research institutions
  interdisciplinary studies, 28
Responsibility center budgeting, 46–47
Retirement
  defined-benefit retirement plans, 72
  early retirement incentives, 71–73
  elimination of mandatory retirement, 65

S

Sabbaticals, 73
Salaries. *See* also Tenure system

containing costs, 48–50
Sanctions, 41
Scholarships, 47–48
Self-assessment, 40–42
Service learning, 13, 34
Specialized accreditation, 40–42
Specialized accreditors, 27
Strategic decision making, 6–8
Students. *See* also Higher education
  academic affairs committee participation, 91
  assessing learning outcomes, 12
  campus life, 33–34
  collaborative learning, 13
  competencies, 14
  engaged learning, 14–15
  enrollment planning and management, 34–36
  experiential learning, 13
  integrative learning strategies, 13–14
  international students, 17
  research projects, 13
  service learning, 13, 34
  student development, 33–34
  study abroad, 14, 17
Study abroad, 14, 17

T

Teaching assistantships, 30–31
Temporary faculty appointments, 69
Tenure files, 76
Tenure system
  AAUP Statement of Principles, 63
  adequate cause terminations, 67–68
  administrative review, 77
  advantages and disadvantages of, 64–65
  alternatives to, 73–74
  decision-making tensions, 5
  early retirement incentives, 71–73
  grievance procedures, 77
  levels of recommendation, 76
  mandatory retirement elimination and, 65
  mid-service review, 76
  nature of appointments, 75
  part-time faculty and, 69–70
  peer review, 76
  performance feedback, 75
  policy reviews, 66–68
  portfolios, 76
  post-tenure review, 70–71
  process and procedures, 74–78
  promotion and, 78
  provisional period, 75
  quotas, 68–69

temporary appointments and, 69
tenure files, 76
TIAA-CREF, 72
Trustees
    authority of, 95–97
    curriculum content decisions, 54–55, 93–94
    decision-making process, 7–8, 53–60
    monitoring faculty policies and procedures,
    80–81
    responsibilities of, 51–60, 94–95
    role in academic programs, 21–22, 25
Trusteeship magazine, 91
Tuition revenues, 47–48

U
United States Department of Education, 41
Universal higher education, 11–12
Universities. See Higher education

V
Volunteer service, 13, 34